Beginning Medical Law

Whether you're new to higher education, coming to legal study for the first time or just wondering what Medical Law is all about, **Beginning Medical Law** is the ideal introduction to help you hit the ground running. Starting with the basics and an overview of each topic, it will help you come to terms with the structure, themes and issues of the subject so that you can begin your Medical Law module with confidence.

Adopting a clear and simple approach with legal vocabulary carefully clarified, Claudia Carr breaks the subject of Medical Law down using practical everyday examples to make it understandable for anyone, whatever their background. Diagrams and flowcharts simplify complex issues, important cases are identified and explained and on-the-spot questions help you recognise potential issues or debates within the law so that you can contribute in classes with confidence.

Beginning Medical Law is an ideal first introduction to the subject for LLB, GDL or ILEX and especially international students, those enrolled on distance learning courses or on other degree programmes.

Claudia Carr is a lecturer at the University of Hertfordshire and module leader of Medical Law and Ethics. She is the author of *Unlocking Medical Law and Ethics* (published 2014) and *Course Notes: Medical Law and Ethics* (published 2012). She is also a co-author of *Beginning Criminal Law* (published March 2013).

Beginning the Law

A new introductory series designed to help you master the basics and progress with confidence.

www.routledge.com/cw/beginningthelaw

Medical Law

CLAUDIA CARR

Routledge
Taylor & Francis Group

LONDON AND NEW YORK

First published 2015
by Routledge
2 Park Square, Milton Park, Abingdon, Oxon OX14 4RN

and by Routledge
711 Third Avenue, New York, NY 10017

Routledge is an imprint of the Taylor & Francis Group, an informa business

© 2015 Claudia Carr

British Library Cataloguing in Publication Data
A catalogue record for this book is available from the British Library

Library of Congress Cataloging in Publication Data has been requested

ISBN: 978-1-138-01301-8 (hbk)
ISBN: 978-1-138-01302-5 (pbk)
ISBN: 978-1-315-79551-5 (ebk)

Typeset in Vectora
by Florence Production Ltd, Stoodleigh, Devon, UK

MIX
Paper from
responsible sources
FSC www.fsc.org   FSC® C013056

Printed and bound in Great Britain by
TJ International Ltd, Padstow, Cornwall

To my husband John Rose, with unconditional love
and endless thanks

'Any love that is not dependent on anything never ceases'.
(Ethics of the Fathers)

Contents

Table of Cases

Table of Legislation

Preface

Medical law and ethics is a relatively new area of law that is growing in complexity by the day. Controversial and contemporary, medical law and ethics often acts as a reflection of our own society, as it is hoped the material in the book does. Throughout the book, the medical professional is referred to as 'he' and the patient as 'she'. While the stereotypical nature of the analogy is regretted, the descriptions are accepted and commonplace.

The book begins with an introduction to ethical theories in order that the reader gains an understanding of the issues that arise in most chapters. Thereafter the area of confidentiality is considered, a fundamental principle in the doctor/patient relationship. From there we move on to resource allocation and consider the Health and Social Care Act 2012 before moving on to a more detailed consideration of medical negligence. Thereafter consent is explored before a chapter devoted to children and the law from a number of different perspectives. Mental health is a large and complex area in itself and it is hoped that the chapter will encourage the enquiring mind to read further. The book then moves on to bioethical issues from birth to death, with a chapter on assisted conception, in which Pre-implantation Genetic Diagnosis (PGD), sex selection, 'saviour siblings' and surrogacy are discussed. These issues are contemporary, ongoing and steeped in ethical argument. After the chapter on abortion we explore organ transplantation, an area brought to life by the question of whether it is ethically acceptable to sell a kidney. The Human Transplantation (Wales) Act 2013 is considered as is the issue of presumed consent, as these are topical issues for the foreseeable future that are likely to directly concern many of us. End of life decisions and assisted suicide are never far from the gaze of the press and the assisted suicide chapter discusses the current law and ethics in as much depth as the book allows. The recent case of *R (Nicklinson) v Ministry of Justice* [2013] EWCA Civ 961, its subsequent appeal together with the Assisted Dying Bill is included in order to chart the development of the law in relation to assisted dying. It is hoped that the reader will find this area of the law fascinating and the book truly engaging.

The law is stated as I believe it to be on 1 August 2014.

Claudia R. Carr

Guide to the Companion Website

www.routledge.com/cw/beginningthelaw

Visit the *Beginning the Law* website to discover a comprehensive range of resources designed to enhance your learning experience.

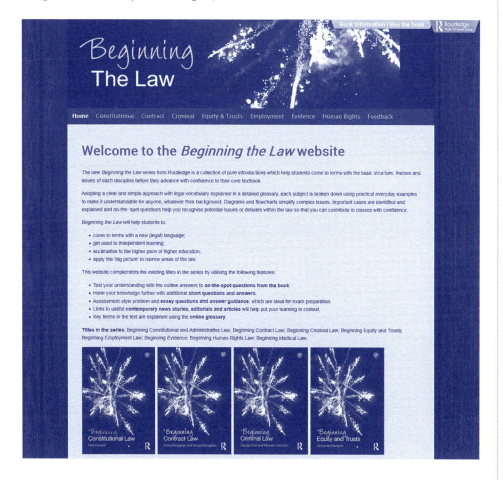

Answers to on-the-spot questions

The author's suggested answers to the questions posed in the book.

Online glossary

Reinforce your legal vocabulary with our online glossary. You can find easy-to-remember definitions of all key terms, listed by chapter for each title in the *Beginning the Law* series.

Chapter 1
Introduction to medical law and ethics

LEARNING OBJECTIVES

By the end of this chapter you should be able to:

- gain a basic understanding of the nature of medical law and ethics;
- demonstrate an understanding of where to locate the law;
- appreciate the importance of reading primary sources.

INTRODUCTION

Medical law and ethics is an area of law which is rarely absent from the media and often appears part of our everyday lives in a way that few other areas of law do. We often hear and read about debates concerning assisted suicide and developments in assisted reproduction that are frequently captured by the tabloid press in a way that does them little justice. When you read this book it is hoped that you will be motivated to read further. By all means, read the current media reports in respected broadsheets such as *The Times* and *The Guardian* newspapers, but do also attempt to gain some academic depth by looking for relevant articles in academic journals such as the *Medical Law Review* and the *Journal of Medical Ethics* to name just two. A true depth of understanding can only really be achieved by reading the primary sources – it is therefore imperative to read the key cases fully. Getting into good habits early is always very advantageous! A similar sentiment applies to the statute law – the *Human Fertilisation and Embryology Act 2008* is surprisingly readable and accessing the original source and reading the relevant sections will give you a far greater understanding of the subject area. Medical ethics or bioethics easily engages one's emotions and it is very possible that you may have already formed your own ideas on subjects such as abortion, assisted conception or end of life issues. It is important, however, to engage with other arguments and academic opinions and then use these arguments to either challenge or reinforce your own opinions.

There is occasionally confusion between the terms 'medical ethics' and 'bioethics' and it is useful to be able to distinguish between the two. Medical ethics describes a more traditional dilemma between the doctor and the patient. For example, Tom visits his GP who advises him that he is HIV+. Should the GP breach the fundamental rule of confidentiality between doctor and patient and inform Tom's wife that he is HIV+ in case her health is also put at risk?

In contrast, bioethics is a more modern term that reflects modern-day ethical dilemmas in the field of medicine. The word bioethics comes from the Greek word *bios* meaning life and *ethos* behaviour. Modern medical advances in technology mean that the ethical dilemmas have become more complex and some decisions can affect society. For example, Ali wants to sell his kidney in order to use the money to support his family. Should he be permitted to? Other issues might include the circumstances in which it is ethically permissible to switch off a patient's life support machine. More topical questions also surround whether assisted suicide should be legalised.

This book will provide the reader with an introduction to some of these areas and the ethical dilemmas will be addressed in the chapters that follow. Some of these issues often raise passionate responses such as 'abortion can never be ethically acceptable' and 'assisted suicide can never be justified on moral grounds'; however, the reader should ensure that whatever opinion is held, the opinion can be justified by reference to an ethical theory and after thorough investigation.

The book is designed to help the reader with an introduction into the various areas of medical law. We begin by exploring ethical theories in order to gain an understanding of the way in which ethical decisions are made. We then embark upon a number of chapters outlining the law. We begin with a chapter on confidentiality. Why is this so important in a doctor– patient relationship and can this ever be breached? We then turn to resource allocation. NHS funds are limited; can every patient expect funding for every treatment they would like? From here we turn to more 'black letter' areas of the law and begin with medical negligence and a discussion of the duty of care owed to patients, and look at what happens when that duty is breached. The following two chapters explain the fascinating area of the law of consent and outline the move from paternalism to autonomy where the competent patient's decisions regarding their medical treatment are concerned. How are incompetent patients treated? From here we move to mental health, a complex area of the law that is stripped back to basics here but which hopefully will encourage the reader to read more on this valuable topic. We then seamlessly move from law to ethics in what can best be described as 'from birth to death'. We begin with assisted conception by considering what is meant by the term 'assisted conception' and the difficulties that can arise, before turning to surrogacy. Next, we encounter abortion law, a highly controversial topic in which we examine both the law and the ethics before moving on to the topical and important issue of organ donation. Our last two chapters deal with end of life issues, beginning with probably the most controversial topic of this decade, the law and ethics of assisted suicide and euthanasia. Finally, we turn to the question of withdrawing and withholding medical treatment from an incompetent patient, another complex legal and ethical issue. It is hoped that this book fulfils its learning objectives in introducing the reader to medical law and ethics.

Chapter 2
Introduction to ethical theories

LEARNING OBJECTIVES

By the end of this chapter you should be able to:

- understand the relevance of ethical theories within bioethics;
- appreciate different ethical theories;
- demonstrate an ability to recognise ethical dilemmas and apply ethical theories in an attempt to solve them.

INTRODUCTION

This chapter will introduce the reader to the main ethical theories that govern bioethical dilemmas. It is important not to concern oneself with which particular ethical theory might apply in a specific bioethical dilemma but to appreciate that the theories you will read below are used interchangeably and seamlessly to resolve complex dilemmas. Towards the end of the chapter, you will encounter theories that are less common but they are included in order to give the reader a more complete picture.

PRINCIPLISM

Principlism is based upon four fundamental principles and represents the most influential set of guidelines to apply to bioethical dilemmas. The four principles are shown in the diagram on page 4.

Autonomy

For some considerable time the courts have recognised the importance of patient autonomy although initially more readily in the USA than the UK. The fundamental nature of patient autonomy was recognised as long ago as 1914 when Cardozo J in *Schloendorff v New York Hospital* stated that 'every human being of adult years and sound mind has a

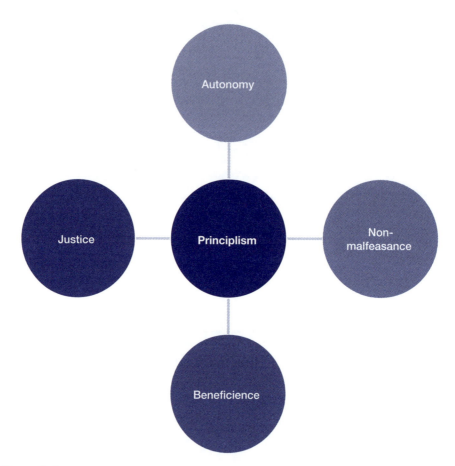

Figure 2.1

right to determine what shall be done with his own body; and a surgeon who performs an operation without his patient's consent, commits an assault'. Today autonomy remains one of the most important and fundamental guiding principles in the care of patients. Beauchamp and Childress define autonomy as 'self rule that is free from both controlling interference by others and from limitations, such as inadequate understanding that prevent meaningful choice' (Beauchamp and Childress, 2001, p. 58).

How is autonomy illustrated in practice? In *Re C (Adult: Refusal of Medical Treatment)*, a case we will look at in further detail in Chapter 6, C, a paranoid schizophrenic, was considered to have sufficient capacity to refuse medical treatment to remove his gangrenous foot. Even though his decision was contrary to medical advice, he had the autonomy to be able to make his own decision. As patients we have the autonomy to decide whether to accept or refuse medical treatment, the only prerequisite being that the person is of full age and is competent to make decisions. Patients are able to refuse medical treatment even if the patient will die as a direct result of that refusal.

Seminal cases have highlighted the importance of patient autonomy. For example, in *Airedale NHS Trust v Bland*, Lord Mustill opined 'If the patient is capable of making a decision on whether to permit treatment . . . his choice must be obeyed even if on any objective view it is contrary to his best interests.' In a similar vein, Lord Goff explained that the

> principle of self-determination requires that respect must be given to the wishes of the patient, so that if an adult patient of sound mind refuses, however unreasonably, to consent to treatment or care by which his life would or might be prolonged, the doctors responsible for his care must give effect to his wishes, even though they do not consider it to be in his best interests to do so.

On-the-spot question

 How important do you consider the principle of autonomy where medical treatment is concerned?

Non-malfeasance

The principle *primum non nocere*, meaning 'above all do no harm', is the foundation stone of medical treatment and non-malfeasance imposes a duty upon the medical professional not to harm others.

KEY CASE ANALYSIS: *McFall v Shrimp 10 Pa D & C 3d 90* [1978]

In this American case, McFall, who was seriously ill, needed a bone marrow transplant from his cousin, Shrimp. Although Shrimp had initially agreed, he withdrew his consent. McFall took Shrimp to court for an order forcing him to give bone marrow, thereby foregoing his autonomy. The principle of not doing harm was in conflict. Where was the greater harm being caused? Would harm be caused to Shrimp, who could be compelled to donate bone marrow against his wishes, or would greater harm be caused to McFall if he were not to receive the bone marrow he needed? The court refused to order Shrimp to donate bone marrow against his wishes and McFall died shortly afterwards. The case, although not binding on any jurisdiction in the UK, underlines some important principles.

On-the-spot question

Do you agree with the court's judgment? It represents a difficult balancing act. Should Shrimp have had bone marrow forcibly extracted? Think of why this would not be the correct course of action even though it would save McFall's life.

Beneficence

Beneficence imposes a positive duty to act in the patient's best interests. Beneficence implies an obligation to do 'good' for the patient but sometimes the boundaries of what is 'good' for the patient can be blurred. For example, if a Jehovah's Witness refuses a blood transfusion, preferring to die than to act against his faith, he expresses an autonomous decision, but if he were to be saved would that be doing 'good' and acting in his best interests? A different issue arises when a doctor cannot treat a patient by prescribing lifesaving or life enhancing drugs due to allocation of resources and problems of 'postcode lottery' (see Chapter 4). In these circumstances, the doctor cannot act in a beneficent manner, the patient's autonomy is not respected and justice is not served.

A more complex and unique situation arose in the case of *Re A (Conjoined Twins)* [2001] a case we explore further in Chapter 7. The conjoined twins were to be separated but where was the greater harm caused? In separating the twins, the weaker and dependent twin would die but separation would give the stronger twin the chance of a normal life. If they were not separated, they would both eventually die. The case illustrates the difficulty with the application of ethical principles; non-malfeasance conveys an obligation not to harm others, but in this instance the weaker twin would die once separated and so acting beneficently is difficult to define.

On-the-spot question

Do you think it is more acceptable to separate twins when there is no doubt that one twin will die from a direct result of the separation?

Justice

The idea of justice means that every patient should receive fair and equal treatment. In practice, this may not be so easy to achieve. Those who are less engaged with society and poorer educated may not be able to access patient care as easily as those who are. Where a patient is recommended medical treatment but due to resource allocation cannot access it, injustice results from the failure to provide equal access to treatment.

On-the-spot question

 Consider your local area or community. Can you identify any evidence of injustice in accessing healthcare?

Figure 2.2

CONSEQUENTIALISM AND UTILITARIANISM

Consequentialism is where the consequences of the action in question are the basis for determining the action's moral value. The more favourable the consequences of an action, the more the act should be encouraged. This ethical principle appears, on the face of it, to be extremely attractive as it simply assesses the value of the consequences.

John Stuart Mill and Jeremy Bentham are often regarded as the most significant proponents of utilitarianism. Bentham, who coined the phrase 'the greatest good for the greatest number of people' wrote *The Principles of Morals and Legislation* in 1789 in which he set out a formulaic approach, referred to as the 'felicific calculus'. Although we are only concerned with the application of the formulae to bioethics, it was applied to many other areas, including economics. The formulae, set out below, can be applied in order to determine the greatest happiness for the greatest number of people.

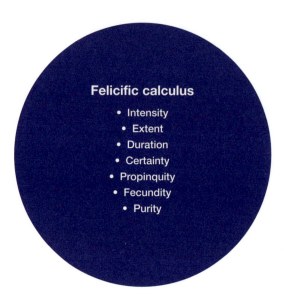

Figure 2.3

Act utilitarianism

Here, the moral value of an act is judged according to its utility and a good consequence is one that provides the most pleasure. It is helpful to apply this hypothetical scenario as this highlights the injustice that this theory can result in. An often quoted hypothetical example is that of five sick patients in hospital, all of whom are in desperate need of organ transplants without which they will die. If the doctor were to kill one healthy visitor, then all the patients would be able to have organs transplanted and all will recover. Let us also imagine that the five patients all have partners and dependent children and all contribute positively to society. In contrast, the healthy visitor has no family, no employment and few friends. This would satisfy utilitarian proponents, as the greatest pleasure is caused to the greatest number of people. The patients all live and return to their happy, useful lives. While one person may die, five will live – a far preferable outcome where utilitarians are concerned. We, however, instinctively know that this would be wrong; an issue that will be returned to shortly.

We can also use the example above to illustrate the application of the felicific calculus which, without explanation, appears largely meaningless.

1   'Intensity' relates to the strength of the pleasure. If a transplant patient were to receive a much needed organ, the pleasure would be immeasurable.
2   'Duration' – one would hope that the organ would not be rejected and, indeed, it is not likely to, but how long the pleasure will last is an unknown factor.
3   'Certainty' – in these circumstances, it would be certain that pleasure would follow from an organ transplant.

4   'Propinquity' relates to how soon the pleasure will occur. If the healthy visitor were to be killed for her organs, propinquity will be satisfied.
5   'Fecundity' relates to the physical nature of the action and the ability to produce further results that would also be satisfied as a transplanted organ will restore the recipient to full health.
6   'Purity' relates to whether the pleasure will be followed by pain. In this example, although more pain would be created, the pleasure derived from the transplant outweighs the pain suffered.
7   'Extent' refers to the extent to which others will be affected by the act. In this situation, the patients will be positively affected and this would outweigh the death of the one healthy visitor.

Rule utilitarianism

Given that the injustice is clearly apparent, rule utilitarianism attempts to provide a balance. This theory adopts a set of rules in order to create the best possible outcome and considers the rules of the action in order to determine its moral acceptability. Once the rule has been followed, the consequences are then determined and the rule that attracts the best consequences is the one that should be adopted.

Rule utilitarianism can also create difficulties. As a rule, it is not ethically permissible to kill. If this rule is to be accepted then we cannot kill another in self-defence even though the law permits us to do so. As a result, weak rule utilitarianism was introduced and this states that where the application of the rule does not create the greatest happiness, it is not necessary to follow the rule. Accordingly, weak rule utilitarianism has more scope to be fair and support the principles of justice than does strong rule utilitarianism, which has more of an absolute function where rules are not to be broken.

Deontology

Deontology focuses on whether an action is intrinsically wrong. Murder is wrong because the act itself is reprehensible rather than the effect of the consequences or the act of murder. Deontology considers whether the act is good or bad, right or wrong rather than the consequences of the action. In our earlier example, Tom, who is HIV+, visited his GP. According to deontological principles, the GP would not breach confidentiality to advise Tom's partner that he is HIV+. The GP's primary concern would be the duty he owes to his patient, including that of confidentiality, rather than the adverse health consequences of not telling Tom's partner.

The most well-known deontologist, Immanuel Kant, argued that the guiding principle in deontology was doing the right action and the motive of the decision maker. Morality derives from a sense of duty, not from a consideration of the possible consequences. In his *Groundwork of the Metaphysic of Morals*, Kant set up a formulae for the guiding principles of deontology which he referred to as the 'categorical imperative'.

The principles are as follows:

- 'Act only according to that maxim whereby you can at the same time will that it should become a universal law.'
- 'Act in such a way that you treat humanity, whether in your own person or in the person of any other, never merely as a means to an end, but always at the same time as an end.'
- 'Therefore, every rational being must so act as if he were through his maxim always a legislating member in the universal kingdom of ends.'

Understanding these principles is not straightforward. Put simply, one can only act in such a way that the law could be applied universally and we should treat others as we would wish to be treated ourselves, not because of the potential consequences but because we have a duty to do so. With regard to the second maxim, this states that we should never act in a way that treats ourselves or others merely as a means to an end.

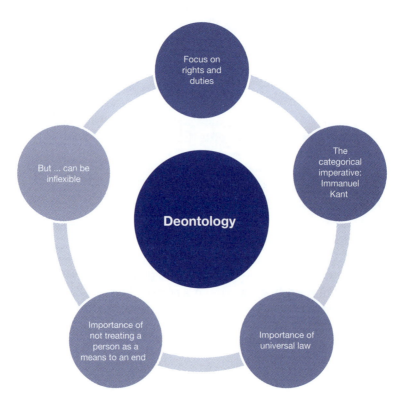

Figure 2.4

Which theory is more attractive?

Utilitarianism was used by the Nazi regime to justify medical experimentation on victims in concentration camps during World War 2 on the basis that the results from experimentation would benefit mankind. Deontology would have no hesitation in considering these actions morally unacceptable and nothing could justify such inhumane activity.

Let us now revert to the earlier example where a doctor has three seriously ill patients – a consequentialist may be able to justify the killing of the healthy visitor in order to save five seriously ill lives, but a deontologist could not. One cannot kill the visitor as it is morally wrong; one cannot use a person simply as a means to an end and, morally, killing one person to save others cannot be condoned.

Earlier, we also considered the case of *McFall v Shrimp*. In terms of consequentialism, the greatest happiness would be caused to the greatest number of people if Shrimp were to be forced to donate bone marrow, as McFall would have a greater chance of survival with the bone marrow transplant than without. In contrast, a deontologist would argue that using a person solely as a means to an end ignores that person's autonomy and is not ethically permissible. Thus, it can sometimes be less than clear where the greatest harm is caused.

Utilitarianism seeks to achieve the greatest happiness for the greatest number of people. However, in trying to achieve the objective, there is a risk of violating a person's right for the alleged good of society and often the fundamental principles of justice and autonomy are disregarded. Another important factor to consider is that if an act is morally acceptable according to its perceived consequences, how can one predict the consequences of an action with any certainty?

However, deontology can be inflexible. If there is a dispute between consequentialists it can be resolved through a discussion of what is the best possible outcome or consequence. A deontologist cannot resolve a dispute; an act is either right or wrong based upon the concept of duties and obligations.

Example

The following is a commonly used example. Sal and Harry are going to a party and Sal has a new dress. She asks Harry 'Do I look nice in this dress?' How would a deontologist reply? How would a utilitarian reply? A deontologist would answer truthfully as deontology is rooted in rights and duties and would tell her she did not look nice, even if that would upset her. A utilitarian would consider how the greatest happiness could be caused and would therefore want her to be happy (and therefore himself as well) and would tell her that she looked nice, even if she did not. How would you approach this scenario?

OTHER ETHICAL THEORIES

Paternalism

Traditionally, the approach of the medical professional was paternalistic, acting as the antithesis to the doctor's autonomy to treat the patient in his best interests often ignoring or overriding the patient's views. In modern medicine paternalism is now considered to be unethical and the case of *Chester v Afshar* finally confirmed this approach in English law where Lord Steyn confirmed that 'in modern law paternalism no longer rules'. Paternalism, however, does still exist and we will see evidence of this in Chapter 7 in the judicial approach to children who refuse medical treatment. There was also considerable evidence of a paternalistic view towards women in labour, prevalent until the case of *St George's Healthcare NHS Trust v S, R v Collins and others* [1998]. There is, however, a prevailing view that there is still considerable evidence of paternalism in modern medicine.

Feminist ethics

Feminist bioethics is an area of bioethics in which the focus is with justice, lack of equality and the oppression of women in healthcare. It may not be immediately apparent how and where this occurs and the following are simply intended to be brief insights.

1   When IVF was introduced, it gave women an opportunity to bear children they otherwise would not have been able to. It has been argued that IVF, while bringing considerable happiness, also oppresses women as the male dominated society and social pressure imposes the obligation on them.
2   There is a limit to the availability of IVF on the NHS. Women who desire IVF and are not in a position to pay for it are victims of a failure of distributive justice.
3   Egg donation for the purposes of human embryonic stem cell research can be contrary to deontological principles. As women can be paid for egg donation, it is likely to be the poorest women who will undergo potentially painful ovarian stimulation for payment. Arguably they are being treated solely as a means to an end.
4   Women are perceived as unequal as traditionally more women occupy the caring role in the medical profession, either as nurses or as familial carers.
5   In many third world countries where women are socially disadvantaged, woman and child prostitutes make up a significant proportion of the population.
6   Many young girls are forced into female genital mutilation. Although now unlawful in the UK, many girls are still at risk and travel abroad during school holidays to undergo the cutting which can leave them with lifelong medical complications and disfigurement. More recent media exposure of FGM in the UK will help to highlight the issue and protect many young girls in the future.

Casuistry

Casuistry dates back to ancient Rome and Greece and applies ethics from a practical perspective by scrutinising each case individually to determine the moral acceptability of an action, using previous cases as an analogy. Casuistry was at its height of popularity in the 1500s. Although not in current vogue, casuistry has a valuable role as it considers dilemmas from a practical perspective.

Virtue ethics

Virtue ethics is an ancient character-based moral theory that emphasises the virtue in the action and decrees that an action is only morally right if a virtuous person would follow it. In contrast to deontology where the duty or right is the foremost consideration, and utilitarianism where one would consider consequences and pleasure, here the primary question is what the virtuous person would do in the situation. Critics would argue that virtue ethics, being entirely dependent on the virtue of the actor, has no boundaries and is too subjective.

Communitarian ethics

Communitarian ethics focuses on the interests of the community rather than the individual. Should a community force vaccinations on all children to avoid spread of a particular disease such as measles? While the community would be protected as a result, communitarian ethics would fail to recognise the autonomy of those who, for their individual and personal reasons, would not wish to receive the inoculation.

SUMMARY

- Bioethical theories can be used to resolve some of the dilemmas posed by modern medicine. They are not used in isolation from each other and as preconceived formulae but as an aide to resolving real life difficult decisions.
- By far the most widely recognised and universally adopted bioethical theory is principlism.
- It is important not to disregard any ethical theory in its entirety as each theory often has a specific role.

ISSUES TO THINK ABOUT FURTHER

- Should childhood immunisation be compulsory for the benefit of the wider community? Support your answer with ethical theories. Which one do you consider prevails in these circumstances?
- Consider why female genital mutilation is unethical. In answering this question, attempt to apply the ethical theories.

FURTHER READING

Beauchamp, Tom and Childress, James (2008) *Principles of Biomedical Ethics*, Oxford: Oxford University Press, 6th edition.

Gillon, R. (1994) 'Medical Ethics: Four Principles Plus Attention to Scope', *British Medical Journal*, 309: 184–8.

Chapter 3
Confidentiality

LEARNING OBJECTIVES

By the end of this chapter you should be able to:

- appreciate the ethical basis for the role of confidentiality and be able to appreciate the role of professional guidance;
- understand the exceptions to the principle that medical records remain confidential;
- demonstrate an understanding of the role of confidentiality in the *Gillick*-competent child.

INTRODUCTION

Doctors are obliged to keep their patients' confidence. A patient must be able to trust his doctor and know that whatever he tells his doctor will remain confidential. If a patient feels that his confidence will be breached, he is less likely to seek medical advice. The duty of confidentiality reflects both deontological and consequentialist ideals. Doctors are duty bound to keep a patient's confidence, but in doing so the greatest happiness for the greatest number of people is also served. It is in the interests of public health if confidentiality between doctor and patient is preserved.

The principle of confidentiality dates back to the Hippocratic Oath which states: 'Whatever, in connection with my professional practice, or not in connection with it, I see or hear in the life of men, which ought not to be spoken of abroad, I will not divulge, as reckoning that all such should be kept secret.'

More recently, the principle of confidentiality has been extended beyond the patient's death. Professional medical bodies such as the BMA unreservedly emphasise the importance of confidentiality, stating that 'Frank and open exchange between health professionals and patients is the ideal and patients need to feel that their privacy will be respected before they can enter into such an exchange' (BMA, 2004).

On-the-spot question

Why is confidentiality between doctor and patient important?

CONFIDENTIALITY AND THE LAW

The law on confidentiality is an equitable common law duty and is not enshrined in statute. The duty of confidentiality that is owed to a patient is not absolute and information can be disclosed if the patient provides their consent to disclosure or if it is in the public interest for the information to be disclosed or if statute states that the information must be disclosed.

The equitable common law duty of confidentiality can be found in numerous court judgments. In *Fraser v Evans* [1969] 1 QB 341 (a non-medical case), Lord Denning MR stated: 'No person is permitted to divulge to the world information which he has received in confidence, unless he has just cause or excuse for doing so'.

Similarly in *Hunter v Mann* [1974] QB 767, Boreham J explained that 'the doctor is under a duty not to disclose, without the consent of his patient, information which he, the doctor has gained in his professional capacity, save . . . in very exceptional circumstances'.

EXCEPTIONS TO THE DUTY OF CONFIDENTIALITY

Express and implied consent

Where a patient provides express consent for disclosure of their medical records, the duty of confidentiality is removed. Even where consent is not given expressly, it can be impliedly granted. For example, where a person is treated by a healthcare team, there is implied consent that medical records will be shared among healthcare professionals.

Public interest

Although the duty of confidentiality is fundamental to the doctor–patient relationship, confidentiality can be broken where it appears in the public interest to do so.

Example

Sohail makes an appointment with his GP. He confides in him that he raped his girlfriend. Can his GP break patient confidentiality and report the conversation to the police? If disclosure is in the public interest, then public interest will outweigh confidentiality.

This principle was illustrated in *W v Egdell* [1990] 1 All ER 835 where the court carefully considered the breadth of the duty of confidence. The court emphasised the importance of confidentiality, but they confirmed the need to weigh up the public interest which favoured disclosure. The court referred to the GMC guidelines on confidentiality where rule 81 states: 'Rarely, disclosure may be justified on the ground that it is in the public interest which, in certain circumstances, such as, for example, investigation by the police of a grave or very serious crime, could override the doctor's duty to maintain his patient's confidence.'

It appears clear that the duty of confidentiality can be overridden by public interest. The situation would be a little different if Sohail was to tell the doctor that he was going to rape his girlfriend when he left. Should the GP tell the police to warn Sohail's girlfriend?

This was precisely the situation that arose in the case of *Tarasoff v The Regents of the University of California* [1976] 17 Cal 3d 358. Although this is an American case and not binding under the law in England and Wales, the decision is interesting as the California Supreme Court decided that a doctor involved in the treatment of psychiatric patients had a duty to warn police if a patient threatened an identified victim. The case has not had any direct effect on the domestic courts; in particular the case of *Palmer v Tees Health Authority* [1999] EWCA Civ 1533 rejected a claim for breach of duty of care on behalf of the health authority following the assault and murder of a young girl by a discharged patient. In order to succeed in a case of this kind, there would have to be a very clear nexus between the patient and the victim and it would have to be reasonably foreseeable that the patient would cause serious harm to the victim.

Table 3.1

Case	Judgment
C v C [1946]	Express consent for disclosure of medical records adequate for doctor to disclose without breaching confidentiality
Tarasoff v The Regents of the University of California [1976]	Protecting the public outweighed the duty of confidentiality
W v Egdell [1990]	No breach of the equitable duty of confidence
Palmer v Tees Health Authority [1999]	Insufficient proximity between the parties to establish a duty of care

Since 2009 the GMC guidance entitled *Confidentiality* has required doctors to disclose information relating to 'a grave or serious crime'. Doctors are now obliged to advise police when they treat a patient who they suspect has been involved in a knife or gun crime. Where doctors suspect that a child is a victim of neglect or physical, sexual or emotional abuse, this information *must* be disclosed if it is believed to be in the patient's best interests or necessary to protect the child from serious harm.

HIV infection

On-the-spot question

Steve visits his GP. He is HIV+. Steve's wife is pregnant and Steve admits to having a number of other sexual relationships. Does the GP break the duty of confidentiality and tell Steve's wife? She is pregnant and her health could be at risk but telling her would undoubtedly damage their relationship.

The answer can be found in the GMC guidance *Confidentiality* (2009). This explains that Steve's GP can (but is not obliged to) tell Steve's wife and other partners if Steve has not done so and cannot be persuaded to do so in order to 'to protect individuals or society from risks of serious harm, such as serious communicable disease'. Steve's GP must be able to justify the reasons for disclosing personal information without Steve's consent and must not disclose the information to anyone who may not be at risk from infection.

Is disclosure of HIV in the public interest?

On-the-spot question

Dr Sal is HIV+. Is it in the public interest for this information to be disclosed?

KEY CASE ANALYSIS: *X v Y* **[1988] 2 All ER 648**

Facts

- Two hospital doctors had been diagnosed with HIV and the information had been disclosed to the press.
- The newspapers accepted that they had received the information in breach of confidentiality but argued that it was in the public interest for the information to be disclosed.
- The doctors sought an injunction to restrain disclosure.

Judgment

It was not in the public interest to break the doctor's confidentiality as the risk of transmission of HIV was insignificant.

KEY CASE ANALYSIS: *H (A Healthcare Worker) v Associated Newspapers Limited and N (A Health Authority)* **[2002] EWCA Civ 195**

Facts

- A healthcare worker tested positive for HIV.
- His employers wished to advise his patients.
- He argued that the risk of transmission was so small that breach of his confidentiality could not be justified.

Judgment

The court accepted his argument that he should not be identified but disclosed the fact that he was a dentist.

H (A Healthcare Worker) v Associated Newspapers Limited and N (A Health Authority) was heard after the introduction of the Human Rights Act in 2000. In the European Courts it was unsuccessfully argued in *MS v Sweden 1997 45 BMLR 133* (ECHR) and *Z v Finland* [1998] 25 EHRR 371 that Article 8 – the right to a private and family life – was breached when medical records were disclosed without the person's consent.

Table 3.2

Case	Principle
X v Y [1988]	Disclosure of the doctor's condition was not in the public interest
H (A Healthcare Worker) v Associated Newspapers Limited and N (A Health Authority) [2002]	Limited disclosure would not breach the health worker's right to confidentiality
MS v Sweden [1997]	Article 8 was not breached by the disclosure of her medical records
Z v Finland [1998]	Article 8 was not breached as the importance of disclosure of the medical records outweighed her right to confidentiality

STATUTORY PROVISIONS

There are some statutes that require disclosure of confidential information of which only a small selection is shown below.

Criminal offences

1   Under the Police and Criminal Evidence Act 1984 where there is reasonable suspicion that a suspect has committed an indictable offence, an application to the court for disclosure of material relating to a person's physical and mental health can be made.
2   The Misuse of Drugs (Notification of and Supply of Addicts Regulations) 1973 requires a doctor who reasonably suspects a person is addicted to a notifiable drug, such as cocaine, to notify the Chief Medical Officer by disclosing the patient's personal details.
3   The Prevention of Terrorism (Temporary Provisions) Act 2000 places a person under a duty to report his suspicion that another is involved in terrorism activities. Although there is a defence of reasonable excuse, this does not extend to the duty of confidentiality.

4   By virtue of the Abortion Regulations 1991 a medical professional who terminates a pregnancy must disclose details to the Chief Medical Officer. In order to preserve her anonymity, her NHS number rather than her personal details are disclosed.

5   Section 168 Road Traffic Act 1988 states that a person must provide the police with information identifying a person who has committed a road traffic offence. Failure to do so is a criminal offence as illustrated in the case of *Hunter v Mann* [1974] 2 WLR 742. Hunter treated a couple who had been involved in a road traffic accident after the vehicle was reported missing. He had advised them to report their involvement in the accident but was charged with not disclosing the information himself. He argued unsuccessfully that the provisions of the Road Traffic Act did not apply to him as he was not acting under the duty of confidentiality.

The medical professional also has other responsibilities. Where a doctor believes his patient is suffering from a condition and should not be driving, he should persuade his patient to contact the Driving and Vehicle Agency (DVA) and, should the patient lack capacity, the doctor should advise the DVA himself. If the doctor believes it is justifiable for the protection of society, he can advise the DVA even where the patient has refused consent to disclosure.

CHILDREN AND CONFIDENTIALITY

In Chapter 6 on consent we explore the case of Gillick (1986), in which a child who reaches an age of sufficient maturity and understanding, has a right to keep their medical information confidential from their parents.

KEY CASE ANALYSIS: *R (Axon) v Secretary of Health* [2008] EWHC 372 (Admin)

Facts

• Mrs Axon sought judicial review of the 2004 Department of Health guidance.

• First, she argued that the duty of confidence owed by medical professionals to a child on matters related to sexual activity was subject to parental knowledge.

• Second, she argued that *Gillick* had to be read in light of Article 8 (the right to a private and family life), which included the right to be advised of treatment involving contraception, sexually transmitted infections and abortions where a child under 16 was concerned.

Judgment

- *Gillick* was to be applied in all cases involving advice and treatment to children. This included contraception, sexually transmitted infections and abortion.
- Where a child was *Gillick* competent, there was a duty of confidence between the doctor and the child, which excluded the parent, and Article 8 could not be engaged.
- Where a child under 16 had capacity to consent, the duty of confidence had to be respected.

ISSUES TO THINK ABOUT FURTHER

- Is it ethically justifiable for a doctor to breach a patient's confidentiality or should this fundamental principle override all exceptions?

SUMMARY

- Confidentiality is a fundamental principle in the relationship between doctor and patient.
- A patient may be reluctant to confide in their doctor if they think that the doctor might breach their confidence.
- This would have an adverse effect on public health.
- There are some circumstances where either the public interest or statutory provisions confirm that confidentiality can be breached.
- A *Gillick*-competent child has a right to confidentiality.

FURTHER READING

British Medical Association (2004) *Confidentiality as Part of a Bigger Picture*.

General Medical Council (October 2009) *Confidentiality: Guidance for Doctors*.

Chapter 4
Resource allocation

LEARNING OBJECTIVES

By the end of the chapter you should be able to:

- appreciate the reality of resource allocation;
- understand the relevance of the QALY;
- understand the judicial approach towards cases of judicial review;
- appreciate the application of the exceptionality criteria.

INTRODUCTION

In this chapter we consider how and why rationing of medical services takes place. Resource allocation or rationing is a reflection of reality. There are simply insufficient funds, regardless of which government is holding the purse strings, to finance every patient's medical needs, even where there is every clinical indication that it would benefit their health.

UK Public Spending shows that healthcare spending in the fiscal year 2014 was £124.4 billion, 18 per cent of total government spending – in line with previous years and successive governments. The sum far exceeds public spending on education, housing or defence. Ideally, there would be sufficient funds to meet all patients' needs but where would this money come from? Another sector would be adversely affected if greater funds were to be diverted to patient care.

Where resources are finite, it is inevitable that not every patient will receive the treatment they need. In this context rationing refers to where a patient is refused a drug due to lack of available funds, not because it is clinically ineffective. Even within the NHS, there are competing demands for funding and a delicate balancing act needs to be performed.

On-the-spot question

? You are given £1,000 to allocate to healthcare services in one lump sum – where would you allocate it? Antenatal care? Neonatal care? Cancer treatment? You might now begin to appreciate that allocation decisions are not quite as simple as they may first appear.

The unpalatable dilemma faced by resource allocation was noted by Sir Thomas Bingham MR in *R v Cambridge Health Authority, ex parte B* [1995] 1 WLR 898.

> I have no doubt that in a perfect world any treatment which a patient . . . sought would be provided if doctors were willing to give it, no matter how much it cost, particularly when a life was potentially at stake. It would however, in my view, be shutting one's eyes to the real world if the court were to proceed on the basis that we do live in such a world. It is common knowledge that health authorities of all kinds are constantly pressed to make ends meet.

A similar notion was expressed by Dyson J in *R v North Derbyshire HA, ex parte Fisher* [1997] 8 Med LR 327:

> when deciding whether to prescribe treatment to a patient, a clinician has to have regard to many factors, including the resources available for that treatment and the needs of a likely benefit to that patient, as compared with other patients who are likely to be suitable for that treatment during the financial year.

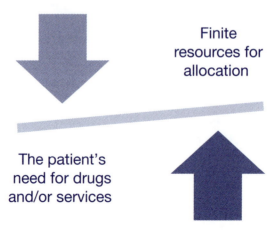

Finite resources for allocation

The patient's need for drugs and/or services

Figure 4.1

From this we learn that rationing of resources is a reality and is a continuing consideration for health service providers. Resources may be finite but patient demand is infinite.

THE NATIONAL HEALTH SERVICE CONSTITUTION

The NHS is free to the general population and according to its constitution (updated 2013) it exists 'to improve our health and wellbeing, supporting us to keep mentally and physically well, to get better when we are ill and when we cannot recover, to stay as well as we can to the end of our lives'.

The NHS Constitution 2009 sets out seven guiding principles. These are not legally enforceable but are commitments between the patient and the NHS.

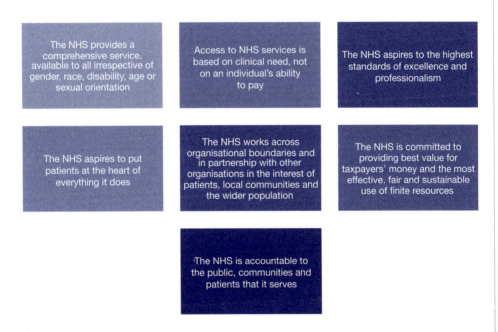

The NHS provides a comprehensive service, available to all irrespective of gender, race, disability, age or sexual orientation

Access to NHS services is based on clinical need, not on an individual's ability to pay

The NHS aspires to the highest standards of excellence and professionalism

The NHS aspires to put patients at the heart of everything it does

The NHS works across organisational boundaries and in partnership with other organisations in the interest of patients, local communities and the wider population

The NHS is committed to providing best value for taxpayers' money and the most effective, fair and sustainable use of finite resources

The NHS is accountable to the public, communities and patients that it serves

Figure 4.2

The principles of the NHS Constitution

The NHS Constitution sets out the rights of patients. These do not appear to be legally enforceable and a patient would not be able to rely on these as a means of legal redress. One right, particularly relevant to resource allocation states that a patient has 'the right to drugs and treatments that have been recommended by NICE (National Institute for Health and Care Excellence) for use in the NHS, if your doctor says they are clinically appropriate for you'. The NHS Constitution refers to 'rights'. Arguably as patients we also have obligations and the NHS Constitution states that patients should take some responsibility for 'good health and wellbeing'.

The Health Act 2009 states that there are bodies within the NHS that must 'have regard to the NHS Constitution'. Some examples of these are primary care trusts, NHS trusts, the Independent Regulator of NHS Foundation Trusts and the Care Quality Commission. The meaning of 'having regard to' is not defined, but there is no statutory obligation to adhere to the NHS Constitution.

The role of the National Institute for Health and Care Excellence (NICE)

There has always been an assurance that healthcare would be accessible to all but the reality of 'postcode lotteries' has never been far from the news headlines. There have been many instances where a patient on one street has been able to receive expensive drugs from their NHS provider but another patient on the next street has been deprived of the same drugs by a different provider. It tends to make a mockery of the principle that all should be equal in the NHS.

NICE was established in April 1999 as the National Institute for Health and Clinical Excellence but was renamed National Institute for Health and Care Excellence (NICE) after the Health and Social Care Act 2012. One of its many roles is to ensure that all patients have equal access to medical care and treatment regardless of their location. Their objective is to make the allocation of resources more transparent in order to avoid the 'postcode lottery' syndrome. NICE is still often criticised by the press for failing to approve drugs and/or services due to the cost.

The role of NICE is not simply limited to the allocation of drugs following an economic health analysis (Clinical Guidelines). One of NICE's many roles also includes advising on the use of new technologies (Technology Appraisals) and consideration as to whether procedures are sufficiently safe.

The Health and Social Care Act 2012

The Health and Social Care Act 2012, which aims to overhaul the NHS, was introduced in a climate of controversy. It is often described as being one of the most significant changes to the NHS since its creation in 1948, with an aim to create an NHS that is a 'coherent, stable and enduring framework for quality and service improvement' with the emphasis on 'priorities and progress in health improvement for all'.

The Act gives groups of GP practices, referred to as clinical commission groups (CCGs) or GPs' consortia, budgets to purchase patient care and the power to set budgets on behalf of local communities. They in turn are supported by the NHS Commissioning Board which authorises CCGs and allocates the resources. Since the GPs' primary role is patient care, this may naturally conflict with an additional role in which allocation of resources also needs to be considered.

Primary care trusts (PCTs) and special health authorities have been abolished and healthcare funds have been transferred to the new CCGs that control 75 per cent of the NHS budget. It is the CCGs' responsibility to decide which provider offers the best healthcare, and this will arguably lead to competition between the private and the public sector. Monitor, a newly established independent health-specific economic regulator, has been established to monitor potential anti-competitive practice. The aim of the Health and Social Care Act is to give patients greater choice and reduce inequality, which in turn will increase GPs' accountability as they respond to their community's needs.

How are resources allocated?

The Quality Adjusted Life Year or QALY is a formula used to calculate the cost-effectiveness of treatment or allocation of drugs.

Figure 4.3

How to calculate the QALY

In order for a healthcare activity to be financially attractive, the QALY must be as low as possible. A basic form of calculation is shown below:

- What is the quality of life before and after treatment? (0 = deceased, 1 = full health.)
- What is the patient's life expectancy before and after treatment?
- Calculate the sum of the life expectancy and the quality of life.
- The result is the QALY.

Each part of a patient's treatment can be calculated in order to reflect the economic value of treatment before it is approved. Arguably, the benefit of QALY-operated resource allocation is that funds are distributed through a utilitarian-style approach, but the QALY approach fails to take into account individual needs and can therefore be unjust by denying fairness.

On-the-spot question

 If you were asked to allocate funds to those who had the greatest need, would you give one patient lifesaving cancer treatment or 1,000 patients cholesterol testing, which could improve the future quality of life for numerous patients?

Criticisms of the QALY approach

1   The QALY approach is discriminatory in nature as elderly or disabled patients who may have the lowest life expectancy and therefore a lower QALY score make allocation of resources less economically attractive.

2   This makes elderly or disabled patients less valued and viewed as a commodity.

3   It is argued that it is the life expectancy of the patient that is taken into account and not the age, but these could be inextricably linked. Nevertheless, a patient of 80 with a life expectancy of 2 years will be considered in the same way as a 40-year-old patient with a life expectancy of 2 years.

4   However, the NICE guidelines 2008 state 'There is evidence that age is a good indicator for some aspects of patients' health status and/or the likelihood of adverse effects of the treatment.' Furthermore, 'There is good evidence, or good grounds for believing, that because of their age patients will respond differently to the treatment in question.'

5   If both a disabled and an able-bodied patient have life expectancies of 5 years with treatment, they should be treated in the same way by the QALY assessment, failing which the disabled patient is discriminated on the grounds of their disability.

6   The NICE guidelines state that consideration should not be given 'on the basis of individuals' income, social class or position in life. Nor should individuals' social roles at different ages affect decisions about cost effectiveness' (NICE, 2008).

7   Where allocation of resources is concerned, what role does patient autonomy now have? There seems to be a conflict between patient autonomy and the subsequent allocation of resources.

On-the-spot question

There are two patients in need of expensive drugs. There are insufficient funds for both. Dylan employs 50 workers in a factory and is married with two children. Marcus is unemployed with no dependants. Who would you allocate the funds to? Once you have allocated the funds ask yourself whether you have discriminated against one patient or the other.

On-the-spot question

Look at the above question again. Dylan and Marcus both have lung cancer. Dylan has been a heavy smoker all his life. Marcus has never smoked. How would you allocate the resources? Has your decision changed from when you first looked at the scenario? How far should we hold the patient accountable for contributing to their own condition?

The complexities of allocation of resources cannot be overstated. Resources that are granted to one patient may often not be given to another. In *Re J (A Minor) Medical Treatment* [1992] 2 FCR 753, Lord Donaldson said:

> the sad fact of life that health authorities may on occasion find that they have too few resources, either human or material or both, to treat all the patients whom they would like to treat in the way in which they would like to treat them. It is then their duty to make choices . . . I would also stress the absolute undesirability of the court making an order which may have the effect of compelling a doctor or health authority to make available scarce resources (both human and material) to a particular child, without knowing whether or not there are other patients to whom those resources might more advantageously be devoted.

The National Health Service Act 2006

The National Health Service Act 2006 imposes upon the secretary of state 'a duty to continue the promotion' of the health service rather than an *absolute duty* to provide a health service. Its duty in Section 2 extends to 'the physical and mental health' and 'the prevention, diagnosis and treatment of illness' and Section 3 explains that the secretary of state has a duty to provide services 'as he considers necessary to meet all reasonable requirements'.

Section 3 was challenged in *R (on the application of JF) v NHS Sheffield Clinical Commissioning Board Group* [2014] EWHC 1345 where the court held that an NHS clinical commissioning group was not in breach of its statutory duty under Section 3 when it declined to provide the same one-to-one care to a patient in hospital that she had previously received in care.

The Act's predecessor, the National Service Act 1977 had been challenged in the courts in *R v Secretary of State for Social Services, ex parte Hinks* [1980] 1 BMLR 93. Here, the court recognised that Section 3 did not impose an absolute duty on health providers to provide every treatment to every patient. Similarly, in *R v North and East Devon Health Authority, ex parte Coughlan* [2001] QB 213 the courts did not find that there had been a breach of an absolute duty to provide medical services. The Court of Appeal said:

> Recent history has demonstrated that the pace of developments as to what is possible by way of medical treatment, coupled with the ever-increasing expectations of the public, mean that the resources of the NHS are and are likely to continue, at least in the foreseeable future, to be insufficient to meet demand.

Judicial review

Judicial review allows an individual to challenge the exercise of power by a public body (the NHS) where it believes that the decision made is one it did not have the power to make, is irrational or unfair. This is referred to as 'Wednesbury' unreasonableness.

In *R v Central Birmingham Health Authority, ex parte Walker* [1987] 3 BMLR 32 the mother of a baby whose operation had been postponed on a number of occasions due to lack of resources sought judicial review of the decision. The court's decision illustrates the difficulty the courts have in considering issues involving resource allocation. The courts refuse to intervene unless the decision-making process regarding the allocation of resources is unreasonable. As Lord Denning explained,

> It is not for this Court, or indeed any Court, to substitute its own judgment of those who are responsible for the allocation of resources. This court could only intervene where it was satisfied that there was a prima facie case, not only of failing to allocate resources in the way others would think that resources should be allocated, but of a failure to allocate resources to an extent which was 'Wednesbury unreasonable' (per Lord Donaldson MR).

A similar sentiment was shared by the courts in *R v Central Birmingham Health Authority, ex parte Collier* (unreported, 6 January 1988) where they said,

> This Court is in no position to judge the allocation of resources by this particular health authority . . . there is no suggestion here that the health authority have behaved in a way that is deserving of condemnation or criticism. What is suggested is that somehow more resources should be made available to enable the hospital authorities to ensure that the treatment is immediately given.

In *R v Cambridge Health Authority, ex parte B* [1995] 1 WLR 898 the Court of Appeal overturned the lower court's decision to ask the health authority to reconsider funding, saying that 'Difficult and agonising judgments have to be made as to how a limited budget is best allocated to the maximum advantage of a maximum number of patients. This is not a judgment that the court can make.'

Table 4.1

Case	Judgment
R v Central Birmingham Health Authority, ex parte Walker [1987]	The court will only interfere if there is a failure to allocate resources reasonably according to the 'Wednesbury' criteria
R v Central Birmingham Health Authority, ex parte Collier [1988]	If the health authority is in accordance with the 'Wednesbury' criteria, the courts will not intervene
R v Cambridge Health Authority, ex parte B [1995]	The health authority had acted fairly and rationally

The exceptionality criteria

We have seen that the courts will not interfere with decisions made by the health provider unless the decision is unreasonable or irrational in accordance with decided principles, accepting that there are funding limitations. It may, however, be possible for patients to argue that their case is so 'exceptional' with regard to the likely benefit of treatment that their case should be funded.

KEY CASE ANALYSIS: *R (Otley) v Barking and Dagenham NHS Trust* [2007] EWHC 1927 (Admin)

Facts

- The patient suffered from cancer.
- She became aware that a drug called Avastin was licensed but not yet available in the UK.
- She paid privately and reacted well to the drug.
- Her specialist applied for the drug from the Trust.
- The Trust refused as her life would not be prolonged to the extent that funding would be cost-effective.
- The Trust said she did not fit the exceptionality criteria.
- She applied for judicial review of the Trust's decision.

Judgment

The application of the exceptionality criteria in this case was both irrational and unlawful. Avastin had proved to be successful and could prolong her life and there was no other treatment which could produce the same result.

Similarly, in *R (Ross) v West Sussex PCT* [2008] 106 BMLR, Ross applied for exceptional funding for the drug Lenalidomide, which had been recommended to him but was not available in his area on the NHS. Without this drug his life expectancy was compromised but the Trust argued that his situation was not exceptional and the drugs were not cost-effective. The courts held that the Trust's decision was both unlawful and irrational, and said that the exceptionality policy was unlawful as a patient had to show that his case was unique, without which he would not be successful.

Table 4.2

Cases	Judgment
R (Otley) v Barking and Dagenham NHS Trust [2007]	The application of the exceptionality criteria to this particular patient was both irrational and unlawful
R (Ross) v West Sussex PCT [2008]	The Trust's exceptionality policy was both irrational and unlawful

Example

Richard suffers from a terminal and rare heart defect and had heard of a new drug that could help his condition. He paid privately for the drug for 6 months and discovered that it significantly improved his quality of life. His consultant is also impressed by the results and asks his Trust to provide Richard with a further 6 months of the drug. The Trust refused to fund the drug, arguing that it was not cost-effective to fund treatment. The only option available to Richard is to apply for judicial review. If the Trust's decision is not irrational or unreasonable, Richard will only be able to gain access to the drugs if he can rely on the exceptionality criteria.

SUMMARY

- There are limited resources and rationing is inevitable.
- The NHS Constitution refers to a comprehensive service where access is based upon a patient's clinical need.
- There is no statutory obligation to adhere to the NHS Constitution.
- A QALY calculates the economic effectiveness of treatment.
- All patients should be treated equally and should not be discriminated against.
- Section 1(1) of the National Health Service Act 2006 refers to 'promotion' of the health service.
- Section 1(2) expresses that the services provided are done so 'free of charge'.
- Section 3 explains the Secretary of State's duty to provide services 'as he considers necessary to meet all reasonable requirements'.
- Judicial review exists as one of the only avenues in which to challenge a hospital's refusal of drugs or services on grounds of resource allocation.
- The courts remain steadfast in their refusal to become involved with executive decisions of allocation of resources.
- The courts will intervene where it is apparent that the 'Wednesbury' criteria have been breached.
- The court will closely consider the exceptionality criteria where unit providers will consider exceptional circumstances as an exception from the general policy of funding limitations.

ISSUES TO THINK ABOUT FURTHER

- Should there be unlimited access to resources? If you think there should be, which other sector of public funding should this come from?
- Do you consider that the QALY is an unfair means of assessing allocation of resources? If you do, try to think of alternative methods of allocating resources.

FURTHER READING

Harris, J. (1987) 'QALYfying the Value of Life', *Journal of Medical Ethics*, 13: 117–23.

Newdrick, C. (2007) 'Low-priority Treatment and Exceptional Care Review', *Medical Law Review*, 15(2): 236–44.

NICE (2008) *Social Value Judgments: Principles for the Development of NICE Guidance*.

Syrett, K. (2008) 'NICE and Judicial Review: Enforcing "Accountability for Reasonableness" Through the Courts?' *Medical Law Review*, 16(1): 127–40.

Follow the link for a Guardian newspaper article on resource allocation:

http://theguardian.com/society/2013/feb/01/nhs-refuses-drug-women-cancer

Chapter 5
Medical negligence

LEARNING OBJECTIVES

By the end of this chapter you should be able to:

- understand when a duty of care is established between the patient and the medical professional;
- appreciate when a breach of duty of care arises;
- appreciate the rules of causation through an understanding of common law;
- demonstrate a thorough understanding of medical negligence.

INTRODUCTION

Imagine you are treated negligently by a medical professional – what is foremost in your mind as a result of your treatment? An apology? An explanation as to why your treatment was wrong and a change in practice to ensure it does not happen again? Compensation? *Making Amends*, a consultation paper that sets out proposals for reforming the approach to clinical negligence in the NHS (Department of Health, June 2003) shows that far from a desire for compensation, the majority of patients want an apology or an explanation for their negligent treatment.

Nevertheless, many patients subsequently sue their health provider in tort for medical or clinical negligence and this costs the NHS millions of pounds per annum. Statistics from the NHS Litigation Authority, (a Special Health Authority responsible for handling clinical and non-clinical cases on behalf of the NHS in England and Wales) show that in 2012–13 £1.3 million pounds was paid out in compensation payments, money that could be diverted into patient care. It is necessary to establish liability in tort in order to successfully sue for negligence, but arguably this perpetuates a culture of blame rather than recognising that medical accidents can and do happen, apologising to the patient and learning from mistakes. *Making Amends* even noted that in some smaller-value claims, the costs of the case outweighed the compensation awarded to the aggrieved patient. Although very few cases end up in court because they are settled before trial, the lack of a public airing of the issues means that although the patient is compensated, lessons are less likely to be learned.

The consultation paper *Making Amends* led to the NHS Redress Act 2006, which intended to address some of the criticisms regarding the handling of lower-value clinical negligence claims. The Act aims to investigate the patient's claim, apologise to the patient where appropriate and take steps to avoid a re-occurrence and, finally, to compensate the patient for the injuries caused. The NHS Redress Act has yet to come into force.

In some cases, where the patient has been treated privately, there will be a contractual relationship between the medical professional and the patient and the patient could sue in contractual law for breach of contract. On very rare occasions, negligence could be considered to be so 'gross' that the defendant may be found to be criminally liable for gross negligence manslaughter (see *R v Adomako* [1995] 1 AC 171*)*. However, by far the majority of cases are carried out under the tort of negligence.

NEGLIGENCE

In order to establish negligence three elements must be proved by the claimant. They are a duty of care; a breach of duty of care; and causation.

Figure 5.1

The injured patient (the claimant) must prove that the defendant owed her a duty of care, which was breached by the defendant by his failure to use reasonable care and skill. The defendant's breach that caused the claimant's injury must not be too remote.

THE DUTY OF CARE

If you have studied tort law you will recall the principle set down by Lord Atkin in the case of *Donoghue v Stevenson* [1932] AC 562, where it was held that a duty of care is established where the injury caused by the other is reasonably foreseeable. The reality is that there is little difficulty in establishing a duty of care between doctor and patient in much the same way as there is a duty between teacher and pupil and train driver and passenger. The principle is demonstrated in the very old case of *Pippin v Sheppard* [1822] 11 Price 400 where it was alleged that the surgeon's acts worsened the patient's condition. The court's view was that 'an undertaking to do a thing . . . creates a liability for negligence and want of due care' so a duty of care naturally flowed.

KEY CASE ANALYSIS: *Barnett v Chelsea and Kensington Management Committee* **[1969] 1 QB 428**

Facts

- Three night watchmen drank tea containing arsenic.
- They began to vomit and attended their hospital's Accident and Emergency Department.
- The doctor failed to see them and told them to see their own GP the following day.
- One man died.

Judgment

Even though there was no pre-existing relationship between the men and the doctor, there was such a close relationship that once the men presented themselves at A and E a duty of care was owed by the hospital.

There are also very occasionally cases where a duty of care has not previously been tested by the courts. In order to help determine whether a duty exists between the parties, the test in *Caparo Industries plc v Dickman* [1990] 2 AC 605 is used and its three elements need to be satisfied.

- Was the damage caused reasonably foreseeable?
- Was the relationship between the medical professional and the claimant reasonably proximate?
- Is it fair, just and reasonable to impose a duty of care on the defendant?

By applying this test, it was possible to establish in the case of *Kent v Griffiths* [2001] QB 36 that a duty of care existed between the ambulance service and the patient to whom they were called.

Duty of care

Table 5.1

Case or statute	Principle or provision
Pippen v Sheppard [1822]	Duty of care established between doctor and patient
Donoghue v Stevenson [1932]	Establishes a tortious duty of care between parties
Caparo Industries plc v Dickman [1990]	Only to be applied in a novel duty of care situation – *Kent v Griffiths*
Barnett v Chelsea and Kensington Management Committee [1969]	A duty of care was owed by the hospital to the patient who attended A and E

CLAIMS FOR WRONGFUL CONCEPTION

The following two contrasting cases illustrate that establishing a duty of care, although initially straightforward, also raises some interesting issues. In *Thake v Maurice* [1986] QB 644, the claimant had a vasectomy but was not warned of the risk of the procedure failing. The claimant's wife fell pregnant as a result of spontaneous reversal and she alleged negligence. Using the test referred to from *Caparo*, the Court of Appeal held that a duty of care existed between the claimant's wife and the defendant as it was reasonably foreseeable that she would be injured (fall pregnant) if the vasectomy failed.

The Court of Appeal held that a duty of care existed between the parties because it was reasonably foreseeable that the wife could become pregnant if the vasectomy failed to be effective. As such, there was sufficient proximity and a duty of care was owed. In contrast, in the case of *Goodwill v British Pregnancy Advisory Service* [1996] 2 ALL ER 161, the defendant had a vasectomy and three years later met the claimant with whom he had had unprotected sexual intercourse. When she fell pregnant, the claimant alleged negligence. In this case, there was not a duty of care as there was an insufficient proximate relationship between the claimant's future partner and the defendant to establish a duty of care and it was not fair, reasonable and just to impose such a duty.

Table 5.2

Case	Principle
Thake v Maurice [1986]	Sufficient proximity between the wife of the patient and the defendant for a duty of care to arise
Goodwill v British Pregnancy Advisory Service [1996]	Insufficient proximity between the claimant and the defendant to establish a duty of care

CLAIMS FOR WRONGFUL BIRTH

'Wrongful births' are those that, had it not been for the defendant's negligence, the baby would not have been born. Clearly a duty of care exists that has been breached and a baby born as a result. The case of *McFarlane v Tayside Health Board* [2000] 2 AC 59 overruled *Emeh v Kensington and Chelsea and Westminster AHA* [1985] QB 1012 and held that the cost of bringing up a healthy baby cannot be recovered from the defendants even though the elements of negligence are entirely satisfied. As a matter of public policy, it seems that since every new birth is a blessing, the law should not compensate the aggrieved party even where the baby was not originally desired. In the latter case of *Parkinson v St James and Seacroft University Hospital NHS Trust* [2001] EWCA Civ 113 the claimant had a disabled baby which, although it would still bring pleasure, was also associated with greater costs. In these circumstances the court held it would be fair, just and reasonable to award the claimant the additional costs that the disability would attract. In *Rees v Darlington Memorial Hospital NHS Trust* [2003] UKHL 52 a disabled woman who was sterilised but then gave birth to a healthy baby was unable to recover additional damages due to the claimant's disability, but did receive a conventional award.

Table 5.3

Case	Principle
McFarlane v Tayside Health Board [2009]	Although negligence was proved, damages were not recoverable where a healthy baby was born as a result of the negligence
Parkinson v St James and Seacroft University Hospital NHS Trust [2001]	Where a disabled baby was born, the additional cost connected to the disability could be recovered
Rees v Darlington Memorial Hospital NHS Trust [2003]	Damages in relation to a healthy child born to a disabled mother could not be recovered

WHO ARE THE POTENTIAL DEFENDANTS?

Example

Suzanne is being treated at Westlock NHS Trust for a pain in her right elbow. She requires a small operation to repair a torn tendon. Mr Cable, in error, operates on her left tendon and she is left with some permanent disability. Who could Suzanne sue for negligence? There are three possible defendants:

- Suzanne sues Mr Cable directly.

- More likely, Suzanne sues Mr Cable's employer, Westlock NHS Trust, under the doctrine of vicarious liability, by which the employer is held liable for the acts or omissions of their employees. (In the case of *Cassidy v Ministry of Health* [1951] 2 KB 343, the defendants were held liable for the negligence of the surgeon employed by them.)
- Or, the claimant could sue the provider of the medical services (Westlock NHS Trust), although this would be unlikely and inappropriate in the circumstances.

KEY CASE ANALYSIS: *Bull v Devon Area Health Authority* **[1993] 4 Med LR 117**

Facts

- The claimant was in labour giving birth to twins.
- Following the first twin's birth a more senior colleague was called.
- The doctor was on another hospital site over a mile away and it took him over an hour to attend the call.
- The delay caused the second twin to be born with severe brain damage as a result of the delay.

Judgment

Even though the hospital operated from two different sites, the delay was an unreasonable one. The hospital had failed to provide a woman in labour with a reasonable standard of care.

In contrast, although the case of *Garcia v St Mary's NHS Trust* [2006] EWHC 2314 was similar to *Bull* on its facts, the court did not find in favour of the claimant. There was a delay of 43 minutes while the on-call surgeon travelled to the hospital, but the court held that not only was the delay not unreasonable but that the brain damage that the patient suffered would have occurred in any event.

WHO MAY BE SUED?

Table 5.4

Case	Who was liable?
Cassidy v Ministry of Health [1951]	The defendant was vicariously liable for the acts of the surgeon
Bull v Devon Area Health Authority [1993]	The unit provider, the defendant, was liable in negligence for failing their duty of care
Garcia v St Mary's NHS Trust [2006]	The delay was not unreasonable and the unit provider has not breached their duty of care

THE STANDARD OF CARE

KEY CASE ANALYSIS: *Bolam v Friern Hospital Management Committee* **[1957] 1 WLR 582**

Facts

- The claimant suffered from a mental illness and was being treated with electroconvulsive therapy which could induce fits.
- He was not advised of the risks and was not given anything to minimise the risk.
- He suffered fractures to his hips and alleged negligence for failure to advise of the risks and to take necessary precautions.

Judgment

The defendants were not negligent. McNair said they had acted in 'accordance with a practice accepted as proper by a responsible body of men skilled in that particular art'.

In many areas of law, the courts are willing to make allowances for inexperience. In the case of a medical professional, allowance is not made for inexperience as explained by Glidewell J in the case of *Wilsher v Essex AHA* [1987] 1 QB 730 who said that 'the law requires the trainee or learner to be judged by the same standard as his more experienced colleagues' and that if inexperience could be taken into account then it would be relied upon in litigation. The justification for this approach appears to be that an inexperienced doctor always has a more experienced colleague to ask for assistance from.

BREACH OF DUTY OF CARE

Introduction

It is relatively easy to establish a duty of care and we have explored who can be sued. It is more difficult to establish a breach of duty of care, which this part of the chapter now reveals.

The standard of care

It is essential to fully appreciate the dictum of McNair J in *Bolam*. There are two basic principles that come from the judgment:

1   'A doctor will not be liable in negligence if he has acted in accordance with a practice accepted as proper by a responsible body of medical men skilled in that particular art' – this means that a defendant will not be liable if he acts in a way that other equally qualified medical professionals would have done.
2   'A man is not negligent, if he is acting in accordance with such a practice, merely because there is a body of opinion that takes a contrary view'– this means that a medical professional will not be negligent even where there are medical professionals who would not have acted as the defendant did. Therefore, the defendant can avoid liability if there is a responsible body of medical men in the same field of medicine who confirm that the defendant's acts were appropriate in the circumstances.

This second limb of the McNair test was not intended to be as controversial as it soon transpired to be. The interpretation of this test was that it appeared that the medical profession was its own arbiter when cases came before the courts. Finding a defendant liable in negligence would be increasingly challenging as the defendant would not be negligent simply because there was a professional body of opinion that would not have done as the defendant did. All that the defendant needed to do to successfully defend a

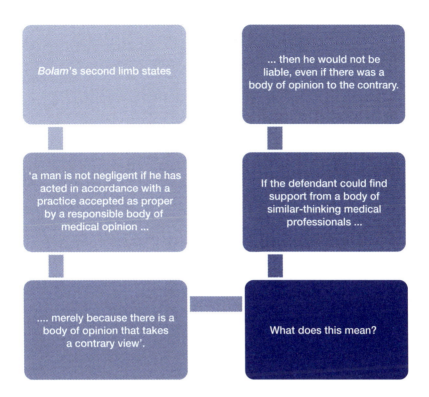

Figure 5.2

claim was to show there was a body of professional opinion that would have, in fact, acted in the way the defendant did.

The impact was widely felt and the test is still applied today. Even though *Bolam* was a first instance case, it was followed by cases such as the House of Lords' cases of *Whitehouse v Jordan* [1981] 1 All ER 267 and *Maynard v West Midlands Regional Health Authority* [1985] 1 All ER 63, which appeared to suggest that it would be almost impossible for the claimant to prove that the defendant was liable in negligence.

Nevertheless, in *Maynard v West Midlands Regional Health Authority* the House of Lords said that negligence cannot be established by simply 'preferring one respectable opinion over another' and Lord Scarman argued that there will often be differences between medical opinion and one cannot draw the conclusion that the medical professional was not negligent simply because his view differs from another. Lord Scarman preferred to assess liability in negligence by whether no other doctor would have done as the defendant did, as this would support the argument that the defendant had not acted with reasonable care.

We have referred to 'a body of medical men skilled in that particular art', but what size should this body be? There is no definitive number but in *Defreitas v O'Brien* [1995] 6 Med LR 108 only a small number of similarly qualified medical professionals would have acted in the way the defendant did. As long as 'there was a responsible body' of medical opinion, it did not matter how big the 'body of opinion' was.

On-the-spot question

? Can you accurately recall McNair J's dictum in *Bolam*? Although *Bolam* has been widely applied, the case of *Hucks v Cole*, a case that was decided in 1968 but was not reported until 1993 rejected the *Bolam* approach, saying that simply because other practitioners would have done as the defendant did is weighty but not conclusive evidence. However, the seminal case of *Bolitho v Hackney Health Authority* attempted to rein the expansion of the *Bolam* test back in.

KEY CASE ANALYSIS: *Bolitho v Hackney Health Authority* [1997] 4 All ER 771

Facts

- The claimant was a 2-year-old boy readmitted to hospital with the childhood respiratory condition, croup.
- Concern grew about his condition and the doctor was called.
- The doctor failed to attend.
- The doctor argued that even if she had attended, she would not have taken the course of action the claimant's argue should have been taken.

Judgment

The doctor breached the duty of care that was owed but the claim failed on causation. Lord Browne-Wilkinson criticised the approach taken by the *Bolam* test.

KEY CASE ANALYSIS: Lord Browne-Wilkinson's dictum in *Bolitho v Hackney Health Authority*

- A doctor should not be able to avoid liability for negligent treatment or diagnosis simply because he can support his approach with a body of professional opinion that would have done the same.
- Lord Browne-Wilkinson referred to references to the terms 'responsible' and 'reasonable' in *Bolam* and said that the use of the adjectives – 'responsible, reasonable and respectable' – shows that the court has to be satisfied that the body of opinion relied upon has a 'logical basis' for that opinion.
- The logical basis referred to means that the experts would have 'directed their minds to the question of comparative risks and benefits and have reached a defensible conclusion on the matter'.

Summary

1   Has the body of expert opinion considered the comparative risks and benefits of the defendant's action?
2   If so, the opinion is capable of withstanding logical basis.
3   In which case, it can be considered responsible, reasonable and respectable.
4   If, on rare occasions, the expert opinion cannot satisfy logical analysis then the judge can conclude that the body of opinion is not reasonable or responsible.
5   But, it would be very seldom that a judge would dismiss an expert's opinion as unreasonable.

Application

1   In *Wisniewski v Central Manchester Health Authority* [1998] Lloyd's Rep Med 223 CA Brook LJ argued that: 'It is quite impossible for a court to hold that the views sincerely held by doctors of such eminence cannot be logically supported at all'.
2   In contrast, in *Marriott v West Midlands Health Authority* [1999] LI Med Rep 23 the court rejected the defendant's expert opinion as being unreasonable.
3   In *M (a Child by his Mother) v Blackpool Victoria Hospital NHS Trust* [2003] EWHC 1744 Silber LJ argued that it would 'very seldom be right' to reject a medical expert's views on the grounds that the court considered it unreasonable.
4   In *Burne v A* [2006] EWCA Civ 24 Ward LJ argued that he did not consider it correct for the judiciary to rely on a common sense approach and reject the experts' views as illogical unless they are given an opportunity to justify their approach.
5   In *Birch v University College London Hospital* [2008] EWHC 2237 Cranston J held that the defendant's expert opinion could only fail to withstand logical analysis where it could not be logically supported at all and suggested that the judiciary would find it very hard to reject medical expert opinion in its entirety.

The *Bolam* test was never intended to act as a method of judicial deference to the medical profession with the medical profession acting as their own arbiters in the court of law. In reality the *Bolitho* test has not had the profound effect that it intended and it is rarely followed.

CAUSATION

Assuming there has been no difficulty in establishing a duty of care that has been breached, we turn next to proving causation. This means that the defendant must be able prove the defendant's negligent act or omission caused the injuries that the claimant alleges on a balance of probabilities (a likelihood of 50 per cent or more).

The first question to ask is 'but for' the defendant's negligence would the claimant have suffered those injuries? Earlier we explored the case of *Barnett v Chelsea and Kensington Hospital Management Committee.* Although there was a breach of a duty of care as the doctor failed to attend the men in the Accident and Emergency Department, the negligence did not cause the claimant's death; the injury the claimant sustained caused his death. Causation was *not* satisfied and the claim failed.

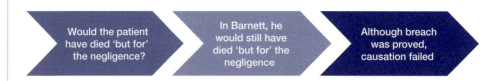

Figure 5.3

Multiple causes

The 'but for' test is easy to apply where there is only one cause of injury. There are, however, many cases where there is more than one potential cause of the claimant's injury and it is not immediately apparent whether the injury was caused by the defendant or by one of the other causes.

KEY CASE ANALYSIS: *Wilsher v Essex Area Health Authority* [1988] AC 1074

Facts

- A baby was born prematurely with a number of complex conditions.
- One condition was due to the negligence of the defendant.
- The baby developed near blindness.
- Was the injury for which he now sought damages caused by the defendant's negligence or by one of the other multiple conditions or causes?

Judgment

Causation failed. The House of Lords held that it was necessary to establish on a balance of probabilities that the defendant caused the claimant's injuries. As the claimants could not prove that the defendant's negligence was the cause of the claimant's near blindness, the claim failed.

This approach produces harsh results for the claimant who will be unsuccessful if it cannot be proved on a balance of probabilities that the defendant's negligent act caused the claimant's injuries. The courts, however, have taken the opportunity to explore more creative ways of determining causation.

KEY CASE ANALYSIS: *Chester v Afshar* [2004] UKHL 41

Facts

- The claimant suffered back pain and consulted Afshar, a neurosurgeon.
- He recommended surgery but did not advise of the 1–2 per cent risk of nerve damage.
- The patient consented to the surgery.
- The risk materialised and the claimant was left partially paralysed.
- She alleged that had she been advised of the risks, she may well have had the operation but would have sought a second opinion first.
- She alleged negligence for the failure to warn of the risks.

Judgment

The claimant was successful. Where a patient was not advised of the risks which materialised in a situation where that patient would not have undergone that operation at that time, she can claim damages for the failure to advise of the risks.

The House of Lords in *Chester v Afshar* delivered what is perceived to be a just result for Mrs Chester as they looked for a more flexible approach to justice. Mrs Chester had not been fully informed of the risks of the operation, although on her own evidence she may have had the operation under exactly the same circumstances but on a different day. The surgeon owed the patient a duty of care to fully inform her of the risk in order that she could provide informed consent. He breached this duty of care and the injuries arose as a direct result of the failure to warn of the risks. In the House of Lords, Lord Steyn said 'the breach by the surgeon resulted in the very injury about which the claimant was entitled to be warned'.

Further developments in the causation test can also be seen in the case of *Bailey v Ministry of Defence* [2008] EWCA Civ 883, which also concerned cumulative causes.

KEY CASE ANALYSIS: *Bailey v Ministry of Defence* [2008] EWCA Civ 883

Facts

* The claimant had suspected gall stones.
* Removal of the gall stones was complicated and she was very unwell.
* Unrelated to any operation, she developed pancreatitis.
* She was transferred to an intensive care unit and then onto a ward.
* She had a drink but was so weak she choked and suffered brain damage before she could be resuscitated.
* The relevant question was, had the Ministry of Defence hospital caused her brain damage, or 'but for' the defendant's acts, would the claimant's injuries have occurred?
* Her weakness had led to the choking, but this was not necessarily the hospital's fault as some level of weakness had been caused by the unrelated pancreatitis.
* The patient argued that the lack of care materially increased the risk of harm.

Judgment

The court of appeal maintained that medical claims should be treated the same as any other claim. It could neither be proved that the lack of care materially increased the risk nor could it be proved that 'but for' the defendant's negligence the injuries would not have occurred. However, in a robust approach to causation, it was held that where 'the contribution of the negligent cause was more than negligible, the "but for" test is modified, and the claimant will succeed'.

Summary of the key principle in *Bailey v Ministry of Defence* [2008]

'If negligence is more than a negligible contribution to the claimant's injuries, it is a material cause. Causation need not be satisfied by a "but for" test.'

Although the test in *Bailey* has been distinguished, it has been applied in the High Court cases of *Canning-Kishver v Sandwell and West Birmingham Hospitals NHS Trust* [2008] EWHC 2384 and followed in the case of *Ingram v Williams* [2010] EWHC 758. In the former case the defendant NHS Trust was held liable for a baby's brain damage as the court held that the hospital's negligence contributed in a manner that was 'more than negligible' in order that the claim could succeed and the defendant be awarded damages.

A FAILURE OR OMISSION TO ACT

Thus far we have considered the different approaches to causation taken by the courts when a defendant acts negligently. Here, we look at the situation in which it is alleged that the defendant has been negligent in failing or omitting to act. In *CJL (A Child) v West Midlands Strategic Health Authority* [2009] EWHC 259, the courts found in favour of the claimant who gave birth to a brain-damaged baby when the obstetrician failed to arrive within a reasonable time and breached his duty of care. However, it becomes considerably more complicated when the failure concerns a failure to act at all. We have already considered the case of *Bolitho* from the perspective of the breach of duty of care; here we consider causation.

KEY CASE ANALYSIS: *Bolitho v City and Hackney Health Authority* [1997] 4 All ER 771

Facts

- The doctor negligently failed to attend the patient even though the nurse had called for the doctor to attend.
- The doctor argued that even if she had attended, she would not have intubated the child as the claimant alleged she should have done and it was not negligent not to do so.
- She argued that her failure to act was not the cause of the child's death.

Judgment

The House of Lords held that the claimant could not prove that the defendant's negligence caused the child's death. Although the doctor should have attended the child when called, it was not negligent not to have intubated as the claimant alleged she should have done. Causation therefore failed.

Example

Ali attends the Accident and Emergency Department of his local hospital. In a tragic accident, he has lost three fingers but he has kept them on ice and hopes to be able to have them reattached. The emergency doctor is very rushed and it takes him several hours to admit Ali. By the time he is seen, it is too late to consider reattaching his fingers. He alleges negligence as he will now be significantly disabled. The hospital breached its duty of care as they did not, it transpires, treat him as speedily as they should. However, medical expert evidence demonstrates that the fingers could not have been reattached in any event. Ali's claim would fail on causation.

LOSS OF CHANCE

Here we are concerned with the approach taken by the courts in which a doctor breaches his duty to a patient and the breach deprives the patient of the chance to make a full recovery.

KEY CASE ANALYSIS: *Hotson v East Berkshire Area Health Authority* [1987] AC 750

Facts

- A 13-year-old boy fell out of a tree injuring his hip.
- He was initially misdiagnosed at the hospital and sent home.
- Five days later he was correctly diagnosed and treated.
- The delayed diagnosis left him permanently disabled.
- Even if he had been correctly diagnosed initially, he could have been one of the 75 per cent of cases that develop the disability he went on to suffer from.
- His claim was for the loss of a 25 per cent chance of making a full recovery from his condition due to the negligent misdiagnosis.

Judgment

The House of Lords held that the original injury caused the disability and unless the claimant could prove on a balance of probabilities that the delayed diagnosis and treatment was at least a material contributory cause, causation would fail. In order to be successful he would have to prove that on a balance of probabilities (50 per cent or more) the defendant materially caused the claimant's injuries.

It is the law that one cannot successfully recover for loss of a chance unless the chances of success exceed 50 per cent, but the approach has been criticised widely. Lord Nicholls in the case of *Gregg v Scott* said

> The present state of the law is crude to an extent bordering on arbitrariness. It means that a patient with a 60% chance of recovery reduced to a 40% prospect by medical negligence can obtain compensation. But he can obtain nothing if his prospects were reduced from 40% to nil.

In this particular case, *Gregg v Scott* [2005] UKHL 2, a negligent correct diagnosis of a tumour meant that the patient's chances of survival were dramatically reduced. Had he been treated promptly, his chances of surviving for a further 10 years were 42 per cent. Following the negligent delayed diagnosis, his chances of surviving a further 10 years had dropped to 25 per cent.

He had to prove that on a balance of probabilities, he would have survived 10 years if the GP had not been negligent in not referring him to a specialist. But, even if the GP had referred him, his chances of surviving another 10 years were only 42 per cent. On a balance of probabilities, he was unable to prove his case and causation failed.

The decision has been criticised. Lord Nicholls explained that 'The loss of a 45 per cent prospect of recovery is just as much a real loss for a patient as the loss of a 55 per cent prospect of recovery' and a loss of chance of making a full recovery due to the defendant's negligence should be actionable.

On-the-spot question

? Stefan is involved in a road traffic accident and damages his arm. With this particular injury there is a 15 per cent chance of residual disability. He attends the Accident and Emergency Department which fails to correctly diagnose the injury until 2 weeks later. He then has the operation that expert opinion concludes he should have had immediately after the accident. Expert opinion also states that given the hospital's negligence he now has a 55 per cent chance of residual disability. With specific reference to loss of chance, is Stefan likely to be successful if he sues the health provider in negligence?

REMOTENESS

Finally, assuming causation has been proved, the claimant must be able to prove that the damage is not too remote. This is unlikely to be an issue in medical law and in *R v Croydon Health Authority* [1998] PIQR Q26 it was held that it was not negligent for the defendants to warn of an abnormality on an X-ray taken for employment purposes. The abnormality affected a pregnancy which she alleges she would not have had, had she known about the abnormality.

DEFENCES

1   *Volenti non fit injuria*, meaning 'to a willing person, no injury is done', is unlikely to be relevant in clinical negligence cases as it infers that the claimant had voluntarily assumed the risk of being injured.
2   *Ex turpi causa* means that an action cannot arise from the claimant's illegal act. It became relevant in *Clunis v Camden and Islington Health Authority* [1998] QB 978

where it was decided that it would be contrary to public policy to allow a claim that only arose due to a criminal offence being committed.

3   Contributory negligence: where a patient has acted contrary to medical advice in such a way that affects their well-being, Section 1 of the Law Reform (Contributory Negligence) Act 1945 can reduce the amount of damages awarded to the claimant reflecting her percentage contribution to the negligence alleged. In *St George v Home Office* [2008] EWCA Civ 1068 it was held that a patient's lifestyle was not a factor to be taken into account when considering the possibility of contributory negligence.

4   Limitation Act 1980: although not specifically a defence, the Limitation Act Section 11(4) provides that a claim for personal injury must be brought within 3 years from the date of the negligent act or omission complained of or date of knowledge, if later. Section 33 provides the court with a discretion to allow a claim to be brought out of time.)

SUMMARY

- There is usually no difficulty in establishing a duty of care.
- The test set down in *Bolam* can make it difficult for a claimant to prove their case.
- *Bolitho* attempted to rein back the interpretation of *Bolam* but the test set down in *Bolitho* is not often applied.
- Causation can be difficult for a claimant to satisfy although the courts have been creative and have, on occasions, made 'claimant-friendly' decisions.

ISSUES TO THINK ABOUT FURTHER

- To what extent do you agree that it is sometimes an uphill struggle for claimants to successfully establish both breach of duty of care and causation?
- How far do you think that the difficulty to claim loss of chance is nothing more than an arbitrary mathematical calculation?

FURTHER READING

Bailey, S.H. (2010) 'Causation in Negligence: What is a Material Contribution?' *Legal Studies*, 30(2): 167–85.

Brazier, M. and Miola, J. (2000) 'Bye-bye Bolam: A Medical Litigation Revolution', *Medical Law Review*, 8(85): 85–114.

Department of Health (2003) *Making Amends – A Consultation Paper Setting Out Proposals for Reforming the Approach to Clinical Negligence in the NHS*.

Woolf, Lord (2001) 'Are the Courts Excessively Deferential to the Medical Profession?' *Medical Law Review*, 9(1): 1–16.

Chapter 6
Consent, capacity and information disclosure

LEARNING OBJECTIVES

By the end this chapter you should be able to:

- appreciate the importance of consent and identify the key elements;
- demonstrate a clear understanding of the provisions of the Mental Capacity Act 2005;
- appreciate the importance of informed consent and the common law development.

THE IMPORTANCE OF CONSENT IN MEDICAL TREATMENT

A patient's consent is essential prior to any treatment. Where a patient does not consent, any physical interference can amount to the tort of trespass to the person (in civil law). It is possible that such interference can even amount to the criminal offence of ABH (actual bodily harm) or GBH (grievous bodily harm), although this would be very unlikely.

The common law reflects the importance of consent. Cardozo J, in the well-known Amercian case of *Schloendorff v New York Hospital 211 NY125* [1914] famously said 'Every human being of adult years and sound mind has a right to determine what shall be done with his own body'.

The above decision did not bind the law in England and Wales but a similar principle was apparent in the case of *F v West Berkshire Health Authority* [1990] 2 AC 1 where Neill J said 'treatment or surgery which would otherwise be unlawful as a trespass is made lawful by the consent of the patient'.

Summary

A patient's consent is the cornerstone to lawful treatment.

INTRODUCTION TO CAPACITY

A patient can only consent to treatment if they have capacity and the Mental Capacity Act 2005 confers a statutory presumption that a person has capacity unless it is proved otherwise. The Act consolidates previous common law decisions and the Mental Capacity Act Code of Practice 2005 states that there are five overriding statutory principles.

1   A person must be assumed to have capacity unless it is established that they lack capacity.
2   A person is not to be treated as unable to make a decision unless all practicable steps to help him to do so have been taken without success.
3   A person is not to be treated as unable to make a decision merely because he makes an unwise decision.
4   An act done, or decision made, under this Act for or on behalf of a person who lacks capacity must be done, or made, in his best interests.
5   Before the act is done, or the decision is made, regard must be had as to whether the purpose for which it is needed can be as effectively achieved in a way that is less restrictive of the person's rights and freedom of action.

THE TEST FOR CAPACITY

Section 2(1) Mental Capacity Act 2005 states that a person will be deemed to lack capacity in relation to a particular matter if:

1   'At the material time he is unable to make a decision for himself in relation to the matter because of an impairment of, or a disturbance in the functioning of, the mind or brain'.
2   'It does not matter whether the impairment or disturbance is permanent or temporary'.

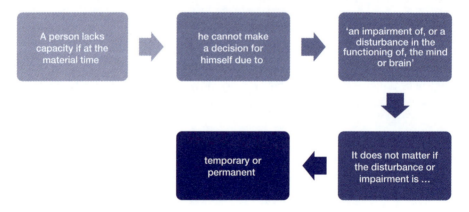

Figure 6.1

'Impairment of disturbance of the mind'

We have seen that impairment or disturbance which can affect a person's ability to make decisions can be temporary. The Code of Practice 4.26 explains that this can include 'acute illness, severe pain, the effect of medication or distress after a death or shock'.

Example

Dylan is injured in a road traffic accident. The ambulance attends and the paramedic gives him morphine to help with pain control. Dylan then says he does not want to go to hospital and 'they are all conspiring against him' and 'the hospital is going to remove his brain and sell it to aliens'. It is possible that the effect of the medication has caused him a temporary disturbance of the mind and, if so, he will lack capacity to make a specific decision (rather than general decisions) relating to his own treatment. However, just because Dylan appears to have made an irrational decision, it does not automatically mean that he lacks capacity.

The Mental Capacity Code of Practice Paragraph 4.12 sets out what amounts to a relevant condition for the purposes of an 'impairment or a disturbance of the mind'. The following list is not exhaustive:

- conditions associated with some forms of mental illness;
- dementia;
- significant learning disabilities;
- the long-term effects of brain damage;
- physical or medical conditions that cause confusion, drowsiness or loss of consciousness;
- delirium;
- concussion following a head injury; and
- the symptoms of alcohol or drug use.

THE COMMON LAW TEST FOR CAPACITY

The case below demonstrates that just because a person appears to make a bizarre or irrational decision, it does not mean that they lack capacity. The test set down in *Re C* now appears in the Mental Capacity Act 2005. Section 2(3) also states that any decision concerning a patient's capacity should not be based on the patient's age, their appearance, their condition or their behaviour.

KEY CASE ANALYSIS: *Re C (Adult: Refusal of Treatment)* [1994] 1 WLR 290

Facts

- The claimant suffered from paranoid schizophrenia and was an inpatient at Broadmoor.
- He was advised to have a gangrenous foot amputated, without which he could die.
- The plaintiff, however, believed he was a famous doctor and he could cure himself.
- He understood the doctor's advice, but rejected it.

Judgment

The court held that there were three criteria for establishing competence:

- being able to comprehend and retain the information;
- a belief in the information; and
- the ability to weigh up the advice in order to reach a decision.

C's decision was irrational but could fulfil the test set down by the courts. Perhaps somewhat satisfyingly for C, his foot recovered without medical intervention.

Key provisions of the Mental Capacity Act 2005

Table 6.1

Section1(1)	Capacity must be assumed unless proved otherwise
Section 1(4)	A person does not lack capacity simply because he makes an unwise decision
Section 2(1)	A person lacks capacity to make a decision 'if at the material time he is unable to make a decision for himself in relation to the matter because of an impairment of, or a disturbance in the functioning of, the mind or brain'
Section 2(2)	The impairment or disturbance of the mind or brain can be temporary or permanent
Section 3(1)	A person lacks capacity (for the purposes of Section 2(1) if he is unable to understand the information relevant to the decision, to retain that information to use, or to weigh that information as part of the process of making the decision, or to communicate his decision

Summary

If a patient satisfies the criteria in Section 3(1) Mental Capacity Act 2005, the patient has autonomy to decide for herself whether to be treated. Where a patient does not have capacity, they will be treated according to their 'best interests'.

Issues to think about

Kyle has been told he is suffering from a rare condition which can kill him. There is an operation he can have from which he could fully recover but he would have to have the operation immediately and the recovery is very slow and not guaranteed. He can understand and retain the information but he is scared and does not know what to do. If he does not have the operation the chances of dying are high. Does he have capacity to decide?

THE SCOPE OF CAPACITY

Capacity must be reached without undue influence or coercion.

KEY CASE ANALYSIS: *Re T (Adult: Refusal of Medical Treatment)* [1993] Fam 95

Facts

- The patient was a pregnant non-practising Jehovah's Witness who was injured in a car accident.
- After a private conversation with her mother, she refused all blood products.
- Her condition deteriorated.
- Other family members applied to the court to overrule her refusal of treatment.

Judgment

The court ordered the blood transfusion as they believed that her refusal had been unduly influenced by her mother and her religious beliefs. Once her capacity had been overridden, the hospital could act in her best interests.

While there is a presumption in favour of capacity, the presumption can be rebutted. The case also demonstrates that the patient's right to decide for themselves is without boundaries. For example, if she were a practising Jehovah's Witness she could refuse medical treatment even where this would lead to her death. In the example of 'Dylan' on page 57, he does not necessarily lack capacity because he thinks that his brain will be taken by aliens. As Lord Donaldson said in *Re T*, 'the patient's right of choice exists whether the reasons for making that choice are irrational, unknown or even non-existent'.

Summary of the judgment in *Re T*

1   There is a rebuttable presumption that every adult patient has capacity to make decisions about their treatment.
2   A decision that is unwise or 'irrational' does not mean that the patient lacks capacity. The patient can refuse medical treatment even where it is certain the patient will die if not treated.

A similar principle was reiterated in *Airedale NHS Trust v Bland* [1993] AC 789, where Lord Goff said

> if an adult patient of sound mind refuses, however unreasonably, to consent to treatment or care by which his life would or might be prolonged, the doctors responsible for his care must give effect to his wishes, even though they do not consider it to be in his best interests to do so.

KEY CASE ANALYSIS: *Re B (Adult: Refusal of Medical Treatment)* [2002] EWHC (Fam) 429

Facts

- Ms B was a 43-year-old woman who was paralysed and dependent on a respirator to breathe.
- There was no hope of recovery.
- She wanted to refuse continuing life-sustaining treatment.

Judgment

Ms B had capacity and was able to refuse life-sustaining treatment. Her life support machine was switched off and she subsequently died.

ISSUES TO THINK ABOUT FURTHER

The law has rejected paternalism and a competent patient can refuse medical treatment even where it can lead to their death. Perhaps it is worth considering whether there is still a role for paternalism in bioethics. One might argue that the law has gone too far in its respect for a patient's autonomy and consequently too far away from the traditional role of a doctor–patient relationship.

- Clarissa is injured in a horse-riding accident and is taken to the Accident and Emergency Department of her local hospital with a broken leg. She is told she needs an operation. She refuses, believing that ancient words of her horse's ancestors will help restore the strength in her leg. Does Clarissa have capacity to refuse medical treatment or should the doctor act in her best interests?
- When a life support machine is switched off, does this satisfy the necessary elements of murder? One might reasonably conclude that it would since the *mens rea* (the mental element) and the *actus reus* are satisfied. However, in *Airedale NHS Trust v Bland* Lord Goff said (obiter) that where a life support machine is switched off, it should be viewed as an omission to act, rather than a positive act and therefore no criminal liability occurs. Is this a justifiable definition or simply a manipulation for the purposes of being able to justify switching off a life support machine?

Summary

1   An adult competent patient can refuse life-sustaining or lifesaving treatment.
2   The refusal must be free from coercion or undue influence.
3   Where there is doubt, the sanctity of life prevails and the patient's refusal will be overridden.

Pregnant women and refusal of medical treatment

It was historically the case that where a woman in labour refused medical treatment, she was found to lack capacity. In the case of *Re MB (Medical Treatment)* [1997] 2 FLR 426 it was likely that she required a caesarean section. She withdrew her consent to the operation due to a needle phobia. The Trust declared that she lacked capacity to decide for herself and she unsuccessfully appealed against the decision. The court held that the presumption of capacity was rebuttable and her phobia rendered her temporarily incompetent. Although the court reiterated the principle that a competent person can refuse medical treatment even though their reasons may be irrational or indeed, for no reason at all, the court added that 'temporary factors such as shock, pain or drugs might completely erode capacity', and that this impairment could temporarily affect a patient's capacity. This paternalistic approach was repeated by the court on a number of occasions until the case below.

KEY CASE ANALYSIS: *St George's Healthcare NHS Trust v S, R v Collins and others* **[1998] 3 WLR 936**

Facts

- The patient had been diagnosed with a condition that threatened both her and her baby's life.
- She refused any medical intervention.
- She was admitted to hospital under section 2 of the Mental Health Act 1983.
- A caesarean section was carried out and a healthy baby was born.
- She appealed against her admission and detention in hospital under the Mental Health Act.

Judgment

The court of appeal held that both the detention and treatment (caesarean) carried out against her wishes were unlawful.

Judge LJ's judgment emphasised the importance of autonomy saying, 'Even when his or her own life depends on receiving medical treatment, an adult of sound mind is entitled to refuse it. This reflects the autonomy of each individual and the right of self-determination.' While this was now an established principle, was the fact that the baby was also at risk a relevant factor? Judge LJ continued

> In our judgment while pregnancy increases the personal responsibilities of a woman it does not diminish her entitlement to decide whether or not to undergo medical treatment . . . She is entitled not to be forced to submit to an invasion of her body against her will, whether her own life or that of her unborn child depends on it. Her right is not reduced or diminished merely because her decision to exercise it may appear morally repugnant.

St George's NHS Trust v S demonstrates that a patient cannot be incompetent simply because '[their] thinking process is unusual, even apparently bizarre and irrational, and contrary to the views of the overwhelming majority of the community at large'.

For example, in *Re SB (A Patient: Capacity to Consent to Termination)* [2013] EHWC 1417 (COP) a 37-year-old woman with bipolar disorder wanted a termination of pregnancy just as the statutory limit of 24 weeks approached. Although she was suffering from a mental disorder within Section 2 of the Mental Health Act, the court held that she had capacity to make this particular decision and a declaration in her favour was granted. Her mental disorder did not mean that she lacked capacity to consent and just because she made a decision that others might regard as unwise or irrational did not mean that she lacked capacity to make that decision.

On-the-spot question

? Charlie is in labour but the baby is in the breech position. She refuses medical assistance as she believes the doctor is really a witch and will poison her baby. She understands that both her and her baby could die. Can the hospital force her to comply?

Summary

- The courts will respect a competent patient's right to make autonomous decisions such as a decision to refuse medical treatment.
- The court will intervene where it believes that a patient temporarily lacks capacity, allowing doctors to take a more paternalistic approach and treat the patient if it is in the patient's best interests.

CONSENT AND INFORMATION DISCLOSURE

Where a patient (or anyone) makes a decision, we need to consider the degree of information that is required in order to make an informed decision. For example, if you are told you need to have an operation, you would want to know more details. Why? When? What are the risks? This last question is the most relevant to our discussion.

It appears that there are two crucial questions. First, how much information must be given to the patient? Second, what happens when insufficient information is given to the patient about their treatment?

Where there has been a lack of information provided to the patient, the defendant could be liable in battery. This is well illustrated in *Devi v West Midlands Health Authority* [1981] CA Transcript 491 (Unreported) where the patient consented to an operation to repair the uterus. The surgeon performed a sterilisation procedure as well, on the basis that he considered it in the patient's best interests. Even though his interest may have been honourable, she had not consented and he was liable in battery.

In a more unusual case (*Appleton v Garrett* [1997] 34 BMLR 2) a dentist treated about 100 patients unnecessarily. Although he had fully explained the reasons for treatment, the explanation was fictitious. The patients had therefore not given real and genuine consent and he was liable in battery.

Battery is, however, not the best way for the claimant to proceed. In *Chatterton v Gerson* [1981] QB 432, the claimant alleged that her consent was invalid as she had not been advised of the risks. The court did not support her claim, stating that it was only necessary to be advised 'in broad terms of the nature of the procedure which is intended, and gives her consent, that consent is real'. The court also indicated that the basis for such an action, where an allegation of lack of informed consent was concerned, was the tort of negligence and not the tort of battery.

Since the patient had consented in broad terms consent was 'real' and there could be no action in battery. Further, the court confirmed that where the claimant is seeking to claim damages for failing to advise them of the risks associated with their treatment, the correct basis for such an action was the tort of negligence (and not the tort of battery).

In *Hills v Potter* [1983] 3 All ER 716 the issue of the amount of information to be disclosed was applied through the *Bolam* test. Here, the doctor 'did not have to inform the patient of all the details of the proposed treatment of the likely outcome and the risks inherent in it but was merely required to act in accordance with a practice accepted as proper by a responsible body of skilled medical practitioners'.

It appears that providing the *Bolam* test was satisfied there was no specific requirement of the amount of information that should be disclosed to a patient.

KEY CASE ANALYSIS: *Sidaway v Board of Governors of the Bethlem Royal Hospital and the Maudsley Hospital* [1985] 1 AC 871

Facts

- Mrs Sidaway was not advised of the 1–2 per cent risk of nerve damage in an operation to help relieve symptoms of neck and back pain.
- The operation was not negligently conducted but the risk materialised.
- She was left severely disabled.
- She alleged that had she been advised of the risks, she would not have had the operation.

Judgment

Mrs Sidaway's claim failed. The *Bolam* test was applied and it was held there was a responsible body of neurosurgeons who agreed that it was acceptable *not* to disclose risk of paralysis to the patient.

It is worth pausing to consider the judgments in more detail. The most compelling is the dissenting judgment of Lord Scarman.

1   Lord Scarman said the 'patient has a right to be informed of the risks inherent in the treatment' and it was not for the medical profession to determine what was in the 'best interests' of the patient.
2   The prevailing question should be whether in the circumstances the risk was such that the patient 'would think it significant if he was told it existed'.
3   But what does significant mean? Lord Scarman explained that it is significant if it is 'material' and material means if 'a reasonable person in the patient's position would be likely to attach significance to the risk'.
4   This suggests that a doctor must always disclose the risk, but this is not the case. Lord Scarman introduced the concept of 'therapeutic privilege', in which the risk need not be disclosed if, in disclosing the risk, it is reasonably considered to be harmful to the patient's psychological health.

Remember that Lord Scarman was the dissenting judgment and although Lord Bridge recognised the importance of what Lord Scarman was advocating, he considered that it was impractical, preferring the application of the *Bolam* judgment, but he also said that there might also be circumstances where 'the disclosure of a particular risk was so obviously necessary to an informed choice on the part of the patient that no reasonably prudent medical man would fail to make it'.

What is a risk that no reasonably prudent person would make? In *Sidaway*, a 1–2 per cent risk did not amount to the degree of risk that no prudent person would make. Lord Bridge indicated that the degree of risk that it would be appropriate to disclose would be one where it was obvious that there was 'a substantial risk of grave adverse consequences' and, in the Canadian case *Reibl v Hughes* [1989] 2 SCR 880, a 10 per cent risk was clearly significant. Lord Templeman also added that disclosure of a particular risk would be obvious where knowledge 'may be special in kind or special to that patient'.

The case of *Sidaway* contains a number of detailed judgments but they have not necessarily been adopted in subsequent cases. In *Gold v Haringey Health Authority* [1988] QB 481 the patient chose to have a non-therapeutic sterilisation operation. She became pregnant and claimed that, had she been advised of the risks of the sterilisation reversing, her husband would have had a vasectomy instead. If you consider Lord Templeman's dictum, one might easily conclude that to be advised of this particular risk was special to this particular patient and since she choose to have this procedure, she would want to be advised of all the risks, but the *Bolam* test was applied without any additions proposed by the Law Lords and it was held that sufficient information had been disclosed.

In *Poynter v Hillingdon HA* [1993] 7 BMLR 192, the courts also decided that there was no duty to advise the parents of a 15-month-old boy of the less than 1 per cent risk of brain damage associated with a heart transplant operation they had consented to.

Table 6.2

Case	Judgment
Sidaway v Board of Governors of the Bethlem RH and the Maudsley Hospital [1985]	The test in *Bolam* standard was applied to information disclosure
Gold v Haringey Health Authority [1988]	Despite compelling dissenting judgments in *Sidaway*, the court applied the *Bolam* test
Poynter v Hillingdon HA [1993]	No duty to inform patient of 1 per cent risk of brain damage

The approach in England and Wales should now be clear. There was no duty to warn a patient of a risk unless it appeared that there was a 'substantial risk of grave adverse consequences'. England and Wales lagged far behind the USA where in the landmark case of *Canterbury v Spence* 464 F 2d 772 (DC) [1972] a patient had not been advised of the

1 per cent risk of paralysis associated with his operation which developed post operatively. On appeal, the court said that 'True consent to what happens to one's self is the informed exercise of a choice' and in order to exercise that choice one needs to be able to evaluate the options and the risks. Given that the average person is not a medical specialist, it is necessary for the patient to require 'a reasonable divulgence by physician to patient to make such a decision possible'.

But how do we decide the amount of information to be disclosed? The court held that 'all risks potentially affecting the decision must be unmasked'. Furthermore, the court continued by setting the information disclosure standard described as the 'prudent patient' standard in which the information to be disclosed is made with reference to whether a reasonable *patient*, rather than the reasonable doctor, would view the information as significant.

Summary

We now have two contrasting approaches, an earlier approach in the USA, which recognises that a patient, in order to exercise her autonomy must be advised of the risk involved in a procedure that the patient would view as significant. The law in the USA is not binding on the law in England and Wales but can be persuasive. In England and Wales the courts took a traditional *Bolam* approach which failed to recognise patient autonomy or the need for informed consent.

What happened next in England and Wales?

There were occasions when the courts appeared to be more patient focused. In *Smith v Tunbridge Wells Health Authority* [1994] 5 Med LR 334 the claimant alleged that he had not been advised of the risks of impotence associated with rectal surgery. The court found in his favour and referred to Lord Bridge in *Sidaway*, stating that it was not reasonable to fail to advise this patient of this particular risk. Only slightly later in *Pearce v United Bristol Healthcare NHS Trust* [1998] 48 DMLR 118, although the claimant was unsuccessful, the court indicated that 'if there is a significant risk which would affect the judgement of a reasonable patient', then the patient should be advised of the risk so that she can decide for herself what course of action she should take.

KEY CASE ANALYSIS: *Chester v Afshar* [2004] UKHL 41

Facts

- Mrs C was not warned of the 1–2 per cent risk of significant nerve damage that could inherently arise from the back operation she had consented to.
- The risk materialised and she was left partially disabled.
- She argued that, had she been advised of the risks, she would not have had the operation that day but would have taken a second opinion.

Judgment

The House of Lords found in Mrs C's favour even though she may have had the operation with Mr A at a later date. There was a duty of care to warn patients of 'possible serious risks' and the defendant failed in this regard.

The judgment is important as it recognises a move from paternalism to embracing patient autonomy and self-determination. Lord Steyn explained that 'in modern law paternalism no longer rules and a patient has a prima facie right to be informed by a surgeon of a small, but well established, risk of serious injury as a result of surgery'.

Table 6.3

Case	Judgment
Smith v Tunbridge Wells HA [1994]	Unreasonable not to advise the patient of this particular risk
Pearce v United Bristol Healthcare NHS Trust [1998]	Necessary to disclose significant risks that would affect the patient's decision whether to consent to treatment
Chester v Afshar [2004]	Duty of care included a duty to warn of possible serious risks

SUMMARY

- A failure to disclose risks has led to liability for trespass to the person, e.g. *Devi v West Midlands Health Authority*.
- However, *Chatterton v Gerson* makes clear that an action for failure to disclose information, on which a decision whether to consent to treatment is based, should be made in the tort of negligence and not in battery.

- In *Sidaway* [1985], Lord Diplock suggested that the level of disclosure required was to be determined by making reference to *Bolam*. The other judges said that the risk should be disclosed if no reasonable medical man could have failed to disclose it. Lord Scarman (dissenting) preferred the 'prudent patient' test.
- A more patient-centred approach was in evidence in *Pearce v United Bristol Healthcare NHS Trust* [1998] where it was suggested that doctors were required to disclose 'serious risk[s] which would affect the judgment of a reasonable patient'.
- In *Chester v Afshar* [2004] the doctrine of informed consent was accepted in a patient-centred judgment. Paternalism no longer had any role in the area of information disclosure.

FURTHER READING

Jones, M. (1997) 'Informed Consent and Other Fairy Stories', *Medical Law Review*, 7: 103–34.

Teff, H. (1985) 'Consent in Medical Procedure: Paternalism, Self-determination or Therapeutic Alliance?', *Law Quarterly Review*, 101: 432–53.

Chapter 7
Consent and the incompetent patient

LEARNING OBJECTIVES

By the end of this chapter you should be able to:

- demonstrate some understanding of advance decisions, lasting powers of attorneys and court appointed deputies;
- appreciate the principle of best interests at common law;
- demonstrate a clear understanding of the provisions of the Mental Capacity Act 2005;
- appreciate the circumstances in which a minor can consent to medical treatment;
- understand the court's approach to a child's refusal of medical treatment.

INTRODUCTION

Here we are concerned with the 'incompetent patient', someone who does not have the capacity to consent to medical treatment. This group of patients can then be divided into three further classes of patient:

- An adult patient who has temporarily lost capacity, for example, a patient who is unconscious.
- An adult patient who has permanently lost capacity, for example, a patient in a coma.
- The minor child.

Before a medical professional can treat an incompetent patient in their 'best interests', they need to check whether the patient has made an advance decision, whether the patient has a lasting power of attorney (LPA) or whether the court has appointed a deputy. If a patient has a debilitating progressive illness, they may well have made provisions for their treatment while they were competent and before they lost capacity.

ADVANCE DECISIONS

This allows a competent person a way to govern their further treatment in the event they lose capacity. Advance decisions (AD) are governed by Sections 24–5 of the Mental Capacity Act 2005, which set down the statutory requirements. The patient must be 18 (or over) and have capacity at the time the AD was made. The AD refers to a time in the future when the patient will lack capacity to consent to treatment. ADs do not normally need to be made in writing and witnessed, unless the advance decision contains a refusal of life saving treatment. In particular, an AD must specify the type of treatment that is being refused and it may also specify the particular circumstances in which the refusal will apply. It can only apply to a refusal of medical treatment and cannot be used to demand treatment (*R (Burke) v GMC* [2005]).

However, an AD may not be deemed to be 'applicable to the treatment' in question if the treatment in question is not dealt with in the advance decision, or the circumstances that the patient is in are different to those in the advance decision, or if the circumstances are different to those which the patient anticipated, and these different circumstances would have affected their decision and there are reasonable grounds for believing this.

Where an AD is not valid or not applicable the doctor should try and take these wishes into account, but treat the patient in her best interests under Section 4 of the Mental Capacity Act 2005. Where the AD is valid and applicable it must be adhered to.

The value of advance decisions

An AD enables a person to exercise autonomy over their future treatment and at a time when they lack capacity. It therefore allows a person to refuse treatment that they do not want. Moreover, it enables a person to exercise the same rights as a person who has capacity – the right of self-determination and of autonomy. It allows us the sense of remaining in control at a time that we are clearly not, providing that our intentions are clearly defined and an AD is not being made for fear of being a burden on others.

The difficulty is that if a person makes an AD today it may not become effective for several years, by which time not only may medical treatment have advanced but life expectancy may be different too. Moreover, our views and perceptions 10 years in the future may be different than they are now.

LASTING POWERS OF ATTORNEY

A patient may wish to appoint a person who can make decisions on their behalf after they lose capacity to consent. The Mental Capacity Act 2005 Section 9 provides that a lasting power of attorney (LPA) can be appointed. If the strict requirements are not adhered to, an LPA will be ineffective. An effective LPA allows the donee to make decisions regarding the patient's treatment, but only those that are in the patient's best interests. A donee cannot refuse consent to a doctor providing life sustaining treatment unless the LPA specifically states it. Acting in the patient's best interests is not necessarily the same as the treatment the patient may have wanted to refuse.

DEPUTIES

A deputy can be appointed by the court if the person lacks capacity in relation to either his personal welfare or property and affairs (Section 16(1) of the Mental Capacity Act).

If a deputy is appointed, he can consent or refuse consent to medical treatment on the patient's behalf. A deputy does not have the power to make decisions in relation to 'the carrying out or continuation of life-sustaining treatment' in relation to the patient.

THE INCOMPETENT ADULT PATIENT

Although the treatment of incompetent patients is now governed by the Mental Capacity Act 2005, the common law prior to the Act is most instructive and must be briefly considered. In Re F (Mental Patient: Sterilisation) [1990] 2 AC 1, a case concerning the sterilisation of an incompetent female patient, the court when searching for a principle to support such an act, relied on the defence of necessity. However, in treating a patient, the court said any act taken 'must be such as a reasonable person would in all the circumstances take, acting in the best interests of the assisted person'.

This may be very helpful but what does 'best interest' mean? The common law introduced quite a wide definition in Re Y (Mental Patient: Bone Marrow Donation) [1997] 2 FCR 172. Here, it was lawful for an incompetent woman to donate lifesaving bone marrow to her sister on the basis that although there was no therapeutic benefit for Y, best interests included not just medical benefit but extended to social and psychological benefit as well.

THE MENTAL CAPACITY ACT 2005

The Mental Capacity Act 2005, which reflects the law today, confirms that any treatment is governed by the best interests test, paying regard to the least restrictive way of achieving this objective. Factors to be taken into account when determining a patient's best interests are set out in the Codes of Practice but are not exhaustive. The views of the patient must be taken into account, as far as is practicable.

1   the person's past and present wishes and feelings;
2   the beliefs and values that would be likely to influence his decision if he had capacity;
3   any other factors that would be relevant if he had capacity.

In order to help assess the above, other people's views will also be taken into account, for example, the power of attorney, donee or other person who has an interest in his welfare.

The case below illustrates 'best interests' in action.

KEY CASE ANALYSIS: *A NHS Trust v DE* [2013] EWHC 2562

Facts

- DE was unable to consent to a vasectomy.
- He had a long-term partner but could not consent to contraception and did not want any more children.

Judgment

The court held that even though it was a non-therapeutic procedure that would affect his life-long fertility, it would be in his best interests to undergo a vasectomy. In doing so, the court departed from the common law decision of *Re A (Medical Treatment: Male Sterilisation)* [2000] 1 FCR 549.

The Mental Capacity Act has been used in a variety of medically related fields.

KEY CASE ANALYSIS: *Re E (Medical Treatment Anorexia)* [2012] EWHC 1639 (COP)

Facts

- E was a 32-year-old anorexic woman who was receiving palliative care only. She had a number of other complex medical issues.

- Although her parents did not want her to die, they only wanted to pursue treatment if there was a reasonable chance of success.

Judgment

The court held she lacked capacity to make decisions regarding her own treatment and that she lacked capacity when she made her AD. There was a slim chance that treatment could help her and, however slim that chance was, the opportunity should be taken.

Table 7.1

Case	Judgment
Re F (Mental Patient: Sterilisation) [1990]	The defence of necessity can be relied upon. Medical professionals can only act in the patient's best interests
Re Y (Mental Patient: Bone Marrow Donation) [1997]	Best interests are not only medical – here it included psychological and social factors
Re A (Medical Treatment: Male Sterilisation) [2000]	It was not in the best interests of the patient to have a vasectomy
Re E (Medical Treatment Anorexia) [2012]	E lacked capacity. There was a slim chance of successful treatment, which was ordered
A NHS Trust v DE [2013]	The court granted a non-therapeutic vasectomy as it was in the patient's best interests

The Mental Capacity Act 2005 and best interests

Table 7.2

Section 1(5)	An act done or decision made must be in the incompetent patient's best interests
Section 1(6)	The act must be conducted in the least restrictive way
Section 4(4)	As far as possible, the patient must be encouraged to participate in the decision-making process
Section 4(6)	The patient's past and present wishes together with beliefs and values must be taken into account
Section 4(7)	Others must be consulted, such as the deputy, LPA and anyone interested in the patient's welfare

On-the-spot question

? Jack, who is 19 years old, lacks capacity. He has recurrent tonsillitis, which now appears resistant to antibiotics. When he suffers from tonsillitis, he is unhappy and miserable. Given that he is unable to provide consent, can his tonsils be removed? Ensure you can support your answer with reference to the Mental Capacity Act 2005.

THE MINOR CHILD AND PATIENT

Section 1 Family Law (Reform) Act 1969 states that a child is anyone under the age of 18. The law divides child patients into three further categories, which are relevant when deciding whether they are able to consent to medical treatment:

1   children aged between 16–18 years;
2   children aged below 16 who are *Gillick* competent; and
3   children aged below 16 who are not *Gillick* competent.

Children between 16–18 years

Section 8 of the Family Law (Reform) Act 1969 creates a statutory presumption in favour of competence where the child is aged 16–18 years. Therefore, a child patient who is older than 16 but younger than 18 is deemed to have sufficient capacity to give a valid consent to treatment. However, the presumption may be rebutted by evidence demonstrating that the child lacks the capacity necessary for making the decision in question. Section 8(1) refers only to the ability of a minor to *consent* to treatment; there is no reference to any ability to *refuse* treatment.

The *Gillick* competent child

The background to the seminal case below concerns a DHSS (Department of Health and Social Security) circular in 1980 which recommended that girls under 16 years of age could lawfully be prescribed the contraceptive pill without their parents' consent or knowledge. The case below was in response to these revelations.

KEY CASE ANALYSIS: *Gillick v West Norfolk and Wisbech Area Health Authority* [1986] 1 AC 112

Facts

- Mrs Gillick, a mother of five girls under the age of 16, sought assurance from her health authority that no medical professional would provide contraception to any of her children while they were under 16, without her knowledge and consent.
- The area health authority declined to give her any such reassurance.
- She then sought a declaration that the DHSS circular was unlawful.

Judgment

The House of Lords refused her declaration. Importantly the court set down five requirements that had to be satisfied before contraception to a child under the age of 16 could be given without parental consent or knowledge.

1   The child under 16 must be able to understand the advice.
2   The doctor is unable to persuade the child to talk to her parents or for him to advise her parents that she requires contraceptive advice.
3   She will continue having sexual intercourse, whether it be protected or unprotected.
4   If she does not receive contraceptive advice, her physical or mental health will be affected.
5   It is in her best interests to receive contraceptive advice and/or treatment without her parents' consent.

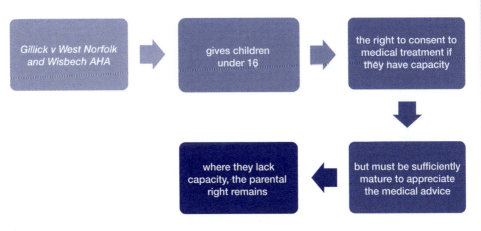

Figure 7.1

It would be a question of fact as to whether the child had sufficient understanding to consent to treatment (whether the treatment was related to contraception or any other treatment) and, until she did, the parental right to make decisions on their child's behalf remained.

The *Gillick* decision was unsuccessfully challenged in the case of *R (Axon) v Secretary of State for Health* [2006] EWHC 37. Where a mature minor has capacity, they have a right not only to autonomy but also to confidentiality.

Example

Adrienne is 15 years old and has sexual intercourse with her boyfriend. She does not want to tell her parents as she believes they will disapprove and stop her seeing him. She is worried about the risk of becoming pregnant even though they sometimes use contraception. She makes an appointment to see her GP without her mother knowing. Her GP encourages Adrienne to talk to her parents but she refuses, worried about any consequences. Adrienne tells her GP she wants to be prescribed the contraceptive pill as she will continue having sexual intercourse with her boyfriend. Satisfied that Adrienne is sufficiently mature to understand the medical advice given, he prescribes her the contraceptive pill and reassures her he will not tell her parents.

Children under the age of 16 who are not *Gillick* competent

Where a child is not '*Gillick* competent', that is, does not have sufficient maturity to understand the advice given to them, they are not able to consent to treatment. However, for a medical professional to lawfully treat a patient, they must have consent. Where a child lacks the capacity to consent, where does this consent come from?

In *Re R (A Minor) (Wardship: Consent to Treatment)* [1991] 4 All ER 177 a 15-year-old girl was considered not to be sufficiently competent to make her own decisions regarding taking anti-psychotic drugs. The question was – how could she be lawfully treated? Lord Donaldson explained that where a child lacks capacity to consent, a child's parent can consent on their behalf, but difficulties could arise where one parent consents and one refuses. It would also be possible for an individual with parental responsibility to consent or even on occasions, the court.

In the slightly later case of *Re W (A Minor) (Medical Treatment)* [1992] 3 WLR 758 a 16-year-old girl with anorexia nervosa refused consent to treatment, relying on Section 8(1) of the Family Law (Reform) Act 1969, and arguing that she had the same rights as an adult to refuse treatment. In an important judgment, Lord Donaldson said that the Act did not apply to a child's *refusal* of medical treatment and that refusal of treatment could be overridden by the court or parental responsibility. In this instance it was the local authority and the court, acting in her best interests, who ordered her to be transferred to a specialised unit.

On-the-spot question

 Does the statutory right to consent to medical treatment convey a right to refuse medical treatment?

The child patient who refuses treatment

KEY CASE ANALYSIS: *Re E (A Minor) (Wardship: Medical Treatment)* [1993] 1 FLR 386

Facts

- A 15-year-old leukaemia sufferer was a Jehovah's Witness who refused blood products on the grounds of his belief.
- The health authority applied for a declaration to lawfully treat him against his wishes.

Judgment

Although the patient had capacity to make general decisions about his treatment, the court allowed the declaration stating that E lacked capacity to refuse lifesaving treatment. He lacked the maturity to fully comprehend 'the manner of his death and the extent of his and his family's suffering'. Ward J stated that the court 'should be very slow to allow an infant to martyr himself'.

The courts have taken a consistent and paternalistic approach. In this respect, in *Re S (A Minor) (Consent to Medical Treatment)* [1994] 2 FLR 1065, the court also overrode a 15-year-old girl's refusal of medical treatment on religious grounds saying 'for her decision to carry weight she should have a greater understanding of the manner of the death and pain and the distress'.

It is unclear whether a court would ever allow a minor child to refuse treatment. It seems that the courts will take every possible step to protect a child from itself until the child reaches the age of majority by raising the bar of the level of understanding so high that it would appear impossible to reach.

On-the-spot question

 Is a minor able to refuse medical treatment? Do you approve of the court's approach?

Treating the child where the parents are in disagreement

This poses a particular ethical problem as in *Re R (A Minor) (Wardship: Consent to Treatment)* [1991] 4 All ER 177 where Lord Donaldson said that the parents disagreed with the doctor's view. Although there is no specific legal issue, as he has the consent of one parent, there are forms of treatment that both parents must agree to. In *Re N (A Child) (Religion: Jehovah's Witness)* [2011] EWHC 373, a 4-year-old child was being brought up by his mother, a Jehovah's Witness, who was separated from his Anglican father. The court had to consider the child's best interests where medical treatment was concerned. Although the mother's religious views were taken into account, in the event that the child needed blood products, the mother would provide the father's details, who would then provide consent.

Treating the child where the parents and the medical team disagree

In these circumstances, the courts have been prepared to override parental refusal and act in the child's best interests. In *Re B (A Minor) (Wardship: Medical Treatment)* [1990] 3 All ER 927 the court overrode refusal for an operation on a Down's syndrome girl who suffered from an operable intestinal blockage. Although the parents' wishes were taken into account, the court, taking the welfare of the child as 'the paramount consideration', concluded that it was in the child's best interests to undergo the operation. A similar decision was reached in *Re C (a Minor) (Medical Treatment)* [1998] Lloyd's Rep Med 1 where the parents of a baby would not agree to discontinue ventilation that was considered futile and where the burden of ventilation did not outweigh the benefits. The court recognised the principle of the sanctity of life, but in this case removal of ventilation was in the baby's best interest. More recently, in *Birmingham Children's NHS Trust v B* [2014] EWHC 531 the parents of a young baby were unable to consent to their baby's urgent heart operation due to their religious beliefs. The parents' refusal was overruled as it was in the baby's best interest to undergo surgery, which would increase his chances of survival.

There is considerable reference to 'best interests' but sometimes what is in a patient's best interests is not always clear. No case better illustrates this difficulty, than the unique case below, which raised complex moral and ethical issues.

KEY CASE ANALYSIS: *Re A (Children) (Conjoined Twins: Surgical Separation)* **[2001] Fam 147**

Facts

- Conjoined twins Jodie and Mary were born.
- Mary was the weaker twin, parasitic on her twin for the blood supply from Jodie's heart.
- Their parents, who were Catholic, did not want them to be separated even though without separation they would both die.
- If the doctors waited until Mary died, a separation at that stage would put Jodie at risk.
- If the twins were separated, then it was clear that Mary would die but Jodie would have a reasonable chance of a normal life.
- The parents wanted to leave it in G-d's hands. The Trust applied to the court for a declaration to separate the twins.

Before we consider the judgment we need to consider two ethical issues. First, what was in Mary's best interests? What was in Jodie's best interests? Mary had very poor health; she was largely dependent on Jodie for her blood supply and had a significantly reduced brain capacity. Separation would kill Mary but would be in Jodie's best interests, giving her the best chance of a normal life. How could the twins' interests be best balanced? It is not acceptable to weigh up which life has greater value, as all life regardless of disability is of equal value and the court had to weigh up both the babies' interests.

In order to justify the separation of the twins when separation would satisfy the legal definition of Mary's murder, the court relied on the defence of necessity having considered the three necessary elements as follows:

1   the act (the separation) is needed to avoid inevitable and irreparable evil;
2   no more should be done than is reasonably necessary for the purpose to be achieved;
3   the evil inflicted must not be disproportionate to the evil avoided.

Summary

Surgery would be in the best interests of the twins, as Mary would be able to die with dignity and be spared the pain and suffering she would otherwise experience and Jodie would be able to live a near normal life. The Trust's declaration was granted and the parents' appeal was dismissed.

Re A (Children) (Conjoined Twins: Surgical Separation) is, of course, almost unique on its facts but the case of *Glass v UK* [2004] ECHR 102 illustrates the extent to which parents can dispute the advice given by their child's treating doctor. Here, David Glass, who was aged 12 at the relevant time, was not suffering from a terminal illness but had complex physical and mental conditions. His condition deteriorated after a minor operation and the doctors put a Do Not Resuscitate order on his notes. The mother took the case through the English courts to the European Court of Human Rights, which found that the hospital's approach to treating David had been a substantial interference with David's Article 8 rights (i.e. the right to a private and family life). The case illustrates the importance of involving the courts where there is a dispute between the treating doctors and parental opinion.

ISSUES TO THINK ABOUT FURTHER

In *Re A*, the courts overrode the parental refusal to separate the conjoined twins. Do you believe that parents should have the final say, even where it is clear that their child will die? The separation of the conjoined twins involved the certain death of Mary. How can this be ethically and legally justified?

SUMMARY

- There is a rebuttable presumption that a child between the ages of 16 and 18 can consent to medical treatment.
- A child under the age of 16 can consent to medical treatment if they are considered *Gillick* competent, that is, they have a sufficient level of maturity and intelligence to understand the implications of the treatment.

- Even where a *Gillick* competent minor can consent to medical treatment, they are unlikely to be able to refuse medical treatment.
- The courts will err on the side of paternalism until a child reaches majority.
- *Re A* illustrates that determining a child's best interest can be extremely difficult where complex moral and ethical issues arise.

FURTHER READING

Coggon J. (2012) 'Anorexia Nervosa, Best Interests and the Patient's Human Right to "A Wholesale Overwhelming of her Autonomy", *A Local Authority v E* [2012] EWHC 1639 COP', *Medical Law Review*, 22(1): 119–30.

Donnelly, M. (2009) 'Best Interests, Patient Participation and the Mental Capacity Act 2005', *Medical Law Review*, 1–29.

Harris J. (2001) 'Human Beings, Persons and Conjoined Twins: An Ethical Analysis of the Judgment in *Re A*', *Medical Law Review*, 9(3): 221–36.

Johnston, C. and Liddle, J. (2007) 'The Mental Capacity Act 2005: A New Framework for Healthcare Decision Making', *Journal of Medical Ethics*, 33: 94–7.

Chapter 8
Mental health law

LEARNING OBJECTIVES

By the end of this chapter you should be able to:

- demonstrate an understanding of the statutory provisions under the Mental Health Act 1983;
- appreciate the common law decisions;
- develop an appreciation of the complexities of the issues.

INTRODUCTION

Mental illness is a vast and complex area of the law and this short chapter will only be able to provide the reader with the briefest of introductions. The Mental Health Act 2007 (MHA) introduced reforms to the Mental Health Act 1983 and made some amendments to the Mental Capacity Act 2005 (MCA), which we have already considered.

Simply because a patient has a mental disorder it does not mean that she lacks capacity. We need only remind ourselves of *Re C (Adult: Refusal of Treatment)* [1994] 1 WLR 290 for confirmation of this principle. The Mental Health Act is only used where the patient has capacity to make a decision about his or her treatment *but* refuses to consent to treatment. One of the main objectives of the Act is to ensure that a person with a mental illness can be treated regardless of their consent where their health and safety or that of others could be affected.

ORDERS UNDER THE MENTAL HEALTH ACT 1983

What is 'mental disorder?'

Section 1(2) of the Mental Health Act 1983 as amended, now defines mental disorder as any 'disorder or disability of the mind'. The Mental Health Act Code of Practice Paragraph 3.3

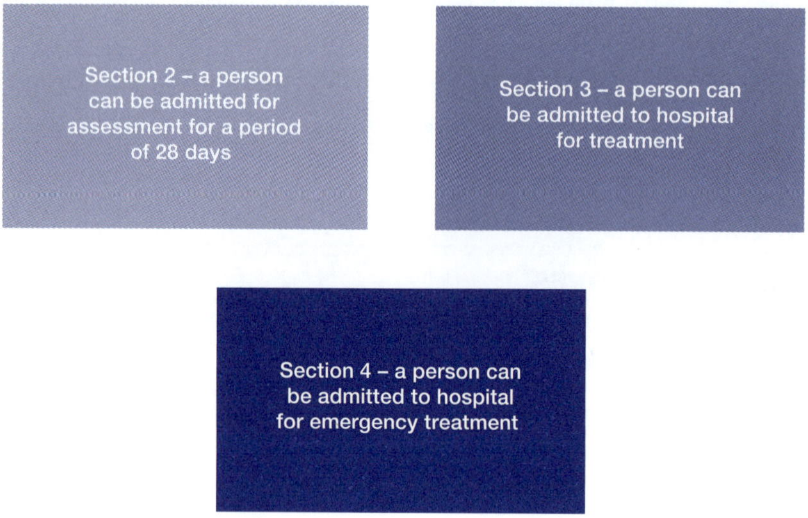

Section 2 – a person can be admitted for assessment for a period of 28 days

Section 3 – a person can be admitted to hospital for treatment

Section 4 – a person can be admitted to hospital for emergency treatment

Figure 8.1

provides some broad examples of what amounts to a disorder or disability of the mind, a few of which are listed below:

- affective disorder, such as depression and bipolar disorder;
- schizophrenia and delusional disorders;
- neurotic, stress-related disorders and somatoform disorders, such as anxiety, phobic disorders, obsessive compulsive disorders, post-traumatic stress disorder and hypochondriacal disorders;
- personality disorders;
- mental and behaviour disorders caused by psychoactive substance use (see below);
- eating disorders, non-organic sleep disorders and non-organic sexual disorders;
- autistic spectrum disorders, including Asperger's syndrome.

Alcohol or drug dependencies are not considered to be mental disorders or disabilities for the purposes of mental disorder under the Act.

Example

Lynne suffers from anxiety and her family believe that she is becoming increasingly anxious to such an extent that they are concerned for her health. Recently, it has appeared that her condition is worsening and she is more depressed than normal. Lynne's family are concerned about the effect that this condition is having on her health. Given this concern, Lynne can be admitted for treatment under Section 2 of the MHA 1983.

Learning disability

'Learning disabilities' are defined as 'a state of arrested or incomplete development of the mind which includes significant impairment of intelligence and social functioning' and are not considered to be a mental disorder unless the learning difficulty leads to behaviour that is 'abnormally aggressive or seriously irresponsible'.

Most applications for assessment or treatment under the Mental Health Act are made by 'approved mental health professionals' who are usually social workers, but could also be a mental health nurse or a psychologist who has had appropriate training.

The Mental Health Act 1983 Codes of Practice

The Codes of Practice are not legally binding but they provide guidance for those who wish to rely on the Act. While the Codes lack enforceability, the House of Lords decision in *R (Munjaz) v Mersey Care NHS Trust* [2006] 2 AC 14 held that the Codes should be applied. There are five guiding principles that should be taken into account when a decision is made under the Act.

- Purpose principle: promoting the patient's recovery and protecting others from harm.
- Least restriction principle: where a patient does not consent, thought must be given to the restrictions placed on the patient's liberty.
- Respect principle: every patient must be respected and there must be no discrimination.

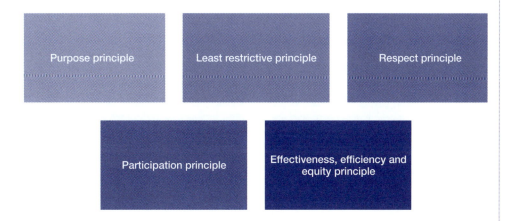

Figure 8.2

- Participation principle: as far as possible, the views of the patient must be taken into account.
- Effectiveness, efficiency and equity principle: the decision taken must meet the needs of the patient in the 'most effective, efficient and equitable way'.

Involuntary admission under the Mental Health Act 1983

Section 2: Admitting a patient for assessment

An application for admission for assessment for treatment without the person's consent can be made for a period of 28 days if a person is suffering from a mental disorder 'of a nature or degree which warrants detention . . . in a hospital for assessment' and it is in the interests of 'his health or safety' or of others. Where a person is detained under Section 2 he has the option to apply to have his case reviewed at a Mental Health Review Tribunal (MHRT) after a 14-day period has elapsed.

In *R v Mental Health Review Tribunal for South Thames Region, ex parte Smith* [1998] 47 BMLR 104 consideration was given to the meaning 'of a nature and degree'. The court said that the two terms were not necessarily linked. A patient's condition may not be of a degree that required detention but the nature of his condition may well justify detention.

Hence, degree refers to the severity of the patient's condition at the time of the hearing and nature involves a more long-term view. The tribunal need not satisfy themselves of both 'nature' and 'degree'; one being sufficient for continued detention.

Section 3: Admitting a patient for treatment

A person can be admitted for treatment without his consent under Section 3 if he is suffering from a mental disorder of a nature or degree that would make it appropriate for him to receive medical treatment *and* it is necessary for his or others health or safety to receive medical treatment *and* appropriate medical treatment is available for him.

Under Section 3 a person can be admitted for treatment for up to 6 months, which can be extended for a further 6-month period.

On-the-spot question

 What are the main differences between Section 2 and Section 3 of the Mental Health Act 1983?

Section 4: Emergency treatment under the Mental Health Act 1983

A person can be detained for emergency assessment for an initial period of 72 hours after which an application can be made under Section 2 or Section 3. An application can be made by either an approved mental health professional or the nearest relative.

Section 136 also permits a police officer to remove a person to a place of safety for a period of 72 hours, if it appears that the person is suffering from a mental disorder and is in need of immediate care or control.

Voluntary admission to hospital under the Mental Health Act 1983

Section 131 of the MHA 1983 allows voluntary admission to hospital for any person who 'requires treatment for mental disorder'. A competent minor aged 16–17 years can also consent to their own informal admission to hospital.

If a patient is voluntarily admitted to hospital, it would follow that they should be free to leave at a time of their choosing. However, there are limitations. Section 5(2) allows a registered medical practitioner to detain a voluntarily admitted patient for up to 72 hours. Section 5(4) allows a nurse to restrain a person from leaving hospital for a period of up to 6 hours if they believe that the person is suffering from a mental disorder to such a degree that it is necessary for her health or safety or for the protection of others that she be restrained from leaving hospital.

The use of Section 5 suggests that there were no procedural safeguards for a voluntarily admitted patient, as the case below clearly demonstrates.

KEY CASE ANALYSIS: *R v Bournewood Community and Mental Health NHS Trust, ex parte L* [1998] 3 All ER 289

Facts

*   L was autistic and was unable to speak.
*   He lived with carers and attended a day care unit at Bournewood hospital.
*   One day he became aggressive and agitated and he was detained under the Mental Health Act 1983.
*   Instructions were given to staff that he should not be allowed to leave although he never attempted to.
*   He could neither consent nor object to his detention.
*   His carers challenged the decision to detain him.

Judgment

The Court of Appeal held that his detention was unlawful as procedure had not been followed but the common law of necessity allowed the hospital to act in the patient's best interests.

In the European Court of Human Rights (*HL v United Kingdom* [2004] 40 EHRR 76) the court held that L's rights were violated. It was a fallacy that a patient such as L was free to leave the hospital. L was under the hospital's control and supervision and even though he did not show any desire to leave the hospital, he was not free to do so, which deprived him of his liberty. The court acknowledged that there were no procedural safeguards to protect a patient against deprivation of liberty

Deprivation of Liberty Safeguards (DoLS)

The Mental Capacity Act Deprivation of Liberty Safeguards (MCA DoLS) were introduced to fill what became known as the 'Bournewood gap' and to provide procedural safeguards for patients who lacked capacity but neither consented nor objected to being admitted and detained in hospital. The MCA DoLS only apply where a patient is deprived of their liberty rather than being restrained or their freedom restricted and only apply to deprivations of liberty in registered care homes and hospitals and do not, at present, apply to patients being cared for at home.

The Mental Health Act 2007 amended the Mental Capacity Act 2005 and Schedule 1A Part 3 now allows a person to be deprived of their liberty where it is considered to be in the patient's best interest. There are six key requirements that must first be satisfied:

- the patient must be at least 18 years of age;
- the patient must be suffering from a mental disorder within the meaning of the Mental Health Act;
- the person must lack capacity;
- it is in the best interests of the relevant person to be deprived of liberty in order to prevent harm to themselves and deprivation of liberty is a proportionate response to the likelihood of the relevant person suffering harm and the seriousness of that harm;
- they must not be detained under the Act or subject to restrictions on their freedom in the community;
- there must not be a valid and applicable advance refusal of the treatment for which the deprivation of the liberty authorisation is sought.

The Mental Capacity Act 2005 Deprivation of Liberty Safeguards Code of Practice 2008 (Paragraph 2.5) provides guidance on the type of acts that can amount to a deprivation of liberty. Such an example could be where staff exercise complete control and effective control over the care and movement of a person for a significant period or staff exercise control over assessments, treatment, contacts and residence.

On-the-spot question

 What is meant by the Deprivation of Liberty Safeguards? With reference to case law, ensure you can fully explain why they were introduced.

Since the introduction of the MCA DoLS, the courts have had the opportunity to consider their application on more than one occasion. In *Hillingdon London Borough Council v Neary and others* [2011] EWHC 1377 the court had to consider whether 'the restraint of liberty was of such a degree or intensity that it amounted to deprivation'. In finding in the respondent's favour, the court held that not only was S deprived of his liberty but there had been a violation of Article 5 of the European Convention on Human Rights.

KEY CASE ANALYSIS: *JE v DE and Surrey County Council* [2006] EWHC 3459 (Fam)

Facts

- DE lacked capacity.
- On occasions he had lived voluntarily at a care home run by Surrey County Council and was living at the care home at the relevant time.
- He had a considerable degree of freedom at the care home.
- He had an ongoing relationship with JE and wanted to leave the care home to return to JE.
- SCC wanted to restrict his residence and stop him returning to JE under the doctrine of necessity.

Judgment

Although he had freedom within the care home, he was deprived of his liberty with respect to his personal choice as to where to live. He was not free to leave in the same way as HL was not free to leave.

The determining factor appears to be whether the patient is free to leave the institution he is residing in and decide for himself where to live. In *P v Cheshire West and Chester Council and another; P and Q v Surrey County Council* [2014] UKSC 19 the Supreme Court confirmed just this point and in allowing appeals from three different patients regarding their deprivation of liberty said that the 'key feature is whether the person concerned is under continuous supervision and control and is not free to leave'. It is likely that this important case will have considerable impact in the future.

Table 8.1

Case	Judgment
Hillingdon London Borough Council v Neary and others [2011]	S's detention was a deprivation of his liberty – Article 5 had been violated
HL v United Kingdom [2004]	Article 5 had been violated as HL had been deprived of his liberty
JE v DE and Surrey County Council [2006]	JE was deprived of his liberty. He was not free to decide for himself where to live
P v Cheshire West and Chester Council and another; P and Q v Surrey County Council [2014]	Appeal successful. The appellants had been deprived of their liberty. Was the person under continuous supervision and control and not free to leave?

Example

Elias has learning difficulties and lives at the local authority care home. He has complete freedom to come and go as he pleases and enjoys visiting the local zoo and the library. He now wants to go and live with his cousin Eddie. The local authority does not want him to leave. Is Elias deprived of his liberty?

TREATING THE MENTALLY ILL

1   Section 57 Mental Health Act 1983: Although rarely used, Section 57 cannot be used without the patient's consent and must be supported by a second opinion together with two other medical professionals. Treatment in Section 57 includes surgery more commonly known as chemical castration.

2   Section 58 Mental Health Act 1983: Section 58 applies to treatment other than that referred to in Section 57. Treatment can be given with the patient's consent or if the patient lacks capacity a second opinion must be obtained. Treatment can include electro-convulsive therapy (ECT). If appropriate, treatment can be given for periods exceeding 3 months.

3   Section 62 Mental Health Act 1983: Section 62 states that Sections 57 and 58 do not apply to treatment which is required immediately in order to save deterioration of the patient's condition or the patient's life and is necessary, but must represent the minimum interference necessary. A second opinion is not needed.

4   Section 63 of the Mental Health Act 1983: Section 63 states that a patient can be given any medical treatment for the condition he is suffering from without his consent. A second opinion is not required. Under Section 63 it is acceptable to use a reasonable degree of force in order to ensure patient compliance. Section 63 has been considered on a number of occasions by the courts and has been widely interpreted.

Section 63 and force feeding

In *KB (Adult) (Mental Patient: Medical Treatment)* [1994] 19 BMLR 144 an 18-year-old anorexic woman had been detained for treatment under Section 3 of the Mental Health Act and was refusing treatment. The question that arose was whether naso gastric feeding was part of the treatment. The court held that feeding via a tube was legitimate treatment within Section 63 because 'relieving the symptoms was just as much a part of the treatment as relieving the underlying cause'. Similarly, in *B v Croydon Health Authority* [1995] Fam 133 a 24-year-old woman with a psychopathic disorder also self-harmed. She had been detained under Section 3 of the Mental Health Act and refused to eat. She applied to the court to restrain the health authority from feeding her without her consent. On appeal, the court held that 'medical treatment' within Section 63 included the condition from which the patient was suffering. Refusing to eat was part of self-harming and feeding by way of a tube was a treatment that could be given without the patient's consent.

Section 63 and caesarean sections

In *Tameside and Glossop Acute Services Trust v CH* [1996] 1 FCR 612 a schizophrenic woman was 37 weeks pregnant and had previously been sectioned under Section 3 MHA 1983. The foetus began to suffer distress and it was possible that a caesarean section might be necessary. There was concern for her mental well-being should the foetus suffer further if she refused a caesarean section. The court held that a caesarean section, even without her consent and with reasonable force if necessary, was within the treatment of her disorder.

The case of *R (on the application of B) v Ashworth Health Authority* [2005] UKHL 20 considered a slightly different issue. Here B was detained for one condition but developed another condition that required treatment. Since he was not detained for the new condition he unsuccessfully argued that it would be unlawful to treat him. More recently, in *Nottinghamshire Healthcare NHS Trust v RC* [2014] EWHC 1317, the court said that it would be lawful to administer a blood transfusion to a Jehovah's Witness who suffered from a personality disorder which caused him to self-harm. The treatment would 'prevent the worsening of the disorder or one or more of its symptoms or manifestations' within Section 63. Of course, as we have already seen, if the patient had capacity, his autonomous right to refuse medical treatment would outweigh sanctity of life.

On-the-spot question

 Morris has been detained under the Mental Health Act. He has decided to refuse all further food. Can he be force fed without his consent?

Cases relevant to Section 63

Table 8.2

Case	Judgment
Re KB (Adult) (Mental Patient: Medical Treatment)[1994]	Forced feeding could be carried out without the patient's consent
B v Croydon Health Authority [1995]	Force feeding was a form of treatment and could be given to the patient without her consent
Tameside and Glossop Acute Services Trust v CH [1996]	Treatment for the patient's condition could also include a caesarean section as this would relieve her symptoms
R (on the application of B) v Ashworth Health Authority [2005]	A patient could be treated for a condition from which he suffered even though it was not the condition for which he was detained
Nottinghamshire Healthcare NHS Trust v RC [2014]	Lawful to treat without his consent as this would prevent a worsening of his disorder

THE HUMAN RIGHTS ACT AND MENTAL HEALTH LAW

Prior to the Human Rights Act (HRA), the courts in *Winterwerp v The Netherlands* [1979] 2 EHRR 387 considered criteria for the lawful detention of those of unsound mind. The criteria emphasises the importance of objectively establishing that the person is indeed suffering from a mental disorder which is of the kind and degree that justifies confinement and that once she is no longer suffering from the disorder, she cannot be lawfully detained.

Since the introduction of the Human Rights Act 1998 the courts must interpret mental health legislation in light of the Human Rights Act and public authorities must ensure that they act in a way that is compatible with the Convention rights. For example, in *Savage v South Essex Partnership NHS Foundation Trust* [2008] UKHL 74 the court held that since there was a real and immediate risk of a patient committing suicide, Article 2 imposed an 'operational obligation' on the Trust to do all that was reasonably expected to prevent the patient from doing so. In *Rabone v Pennine Care NHS Trust* [2012] UKSC 2 which was similar on the facts to the case of *Savage*, the Supreme Court also held that the deceased's rights under Article 2 had been violated where she was able to commit suicide once she left hospital. Just because she was a voluntary patient did not make her any less vulnerable than an involuntarily admitted patient.

The compatibility of Section 2 MHA with Article 5 has also been tested by the courts. In *MH v Secretary of State for Health* [2005] UKHL 60 the court held that since a patient did not have capacity to apply to a Mental Health Review Tribunal herself, she had been detained beyond the statutory 28-day period. In this case, the House of Lords held that Section 2 was not incompatible with the provisions in Article 5(4). However, it was important to ensure that a Convention right was 'practical and effective' rather than 'theoretical and illusory' and if a patient was unable to apply herself to the MHRT then it was important to ensure that she had the assistance she needed.

The use of Article 3 ECHR has led to some interesting judgments. Article 3, an unqualified right, states: 'no-one shall be subjected to torture or to inhuman or degrading treatment or punishment'. In *Herczegfalvy v Austria* [1992] 15 EHRR 437 a hunger-striking prisoner was forcibly fed and given drugs and he alleged violations of his human rights, among them Article 3 which prohibits inhumane or degrading treatment. The ECHR confirmed that there was no derogation from Article 3 but there were circumstances, and this was such a case, where treatment can be justified as a medical necessity and such treatment will not infringe Article 3. The principle was applied more recently in *R (Wilkinson) v Broadmoor Special Hospitals* [2001] EWCA Civ 1545, where the court had to consider whether the hospital could treat the claimant with anti-psychotic drugs without his consent. The court applied Herczegfalvy and held his rights had not been violated. In *R (B) v Dr SS* [2005] EWHC 86, B was a serving prisoner and was detained under the Mental Health Act 1983. He appealed against treatment which he did not consent to. The court applied the principles in Herczegfalvy and accepted that treatment can in some circumstances be considered to be a medical necessity.

Table 8.3

Case	Judgment
Winterwerp v The Netherlands [1979]	Set down the criteria for lawful detention
Herczegfalvy v Austria [1992]	Therapeutic medical necessity acted as a qualification of Article 3
R (Wilkinson) v Broadmoor Special Hospitals [2001]	Article 3 had not been violated
MH v Secretary of State for Health [2005]	Article 5 was violated as she was unable to apply for review to the Mental Health Review Tribunal
R (B) v Dr SS [2005]	Medical necessity can be used to justify treatment. No violation of Article 3
Savage v South Essex Partnership NHS Foundation Trust [2008]	An operational obligation was imposed on the Trust to do all that was reasonably necessary to prevent her suicide
Rabone v Pennine Care NHS Trust [2010]	Operational obligations still applied

DISCHARGE

Article 5 ECHR states that no one shall be deprived of his liberty. Article 5(4) provides that 'the lawfulness of his detention shall be decided speedily by a court' and where his detention is not lawful, the patient must be released. The meaning of the word 'speedily' was tested by the courts in *R (on the application of C) v Mental Health Review Tribunal* [2000] 1WLR 176, where it was held the listing of a MHRT hearing some 8 weeks after the initial application was insufficiently speedy.

Where a patient has been detained under Section 2 or 3 Mental Health Act, they have a right to apply to a MHRT to be discharged (see *MH v Secretary of State for Health* [2005] UKHL 60). A patient should be discharged unless there is evidence that he is suffering from a mental disorder that is of a nature and degree that justifies his detention in a hospital for medical treatment for either his health and safety or that of others.

Conditional discharge

Where a patient is subject to a conditional discharge and the conditions cannot be met so his detention continues, the case *R v Secretary of State for the Home Department, ex parte IH* [2003] 3 WLR 1278 held that his rights under the HRA had been breached. In this case the patient's discharge was dependent on receiving psychiatric supervision and the health authority made every attempt to meet the conditions of his discharge but was unable to. However, the local authority was not under an absolute duty to ensure that it complied with the tribunal's finding – they could only do their best.

Community treatment orders

Supervised community treatment was introduced into the Mental Health Act 1983 by the 2007 Act and allows patients who suffer from a mental health disorder to be treated in the community by way of community treatment orders (CTOs) provided that certain criteria under Section 17 are met. The advantage of CTOs is that they allow the person the freedom of being treated in the community rather than hospital although the person can be recalled to hospital if they fail to comply with the programme of treatment.

SUMMARY

- The Mental Health Act 1983 applies where the patient has capacity but refuses to consent to appropriate mental health treatment.

- Section 2 allows a patient to be assessed where he is suffering from a mental disorder of a nature or degree which warrants detention for assessment, and it is in the interests of the health and safety of the patient or the protection of others.
- Section 3 allows the patient to be detained for a longer period for the purposes of treatment.
- The complexity of some statutory provisions is illustrated in the case of *Bournewood* [1998], as a result of which the Deprivation of Liberty Safeguards were introduced by the Mental Health Act 2007 to the Mental Capacity Act 2005.

FURTHER READING

Dolan, B. and Parker, C. (1997) 'Caesarean Sections: A Treatment for Mental Disorder? *Tameside and Glossop Acute Services Unit v CH (A Patient)* [1996] 1 FLR 762', *British Medical Journal*, 7088: 314.

Fennell, P. (1998) 'Doctor Knows Best? Therapeutic Detention under Common Law, the Mental Health Act and the European Convention', *Medical Law Review*, 6: 322.

Chapter 9
Assisted conception

LEARNING OBJECTIVES

By the end of this chapter you should be able to:

- understand the meaning and relevance of assisted conception;
- demonstrate a clear understanding of the provisions of the Human Fertilisation and Embryology Act 2008;
- understand both the legal provisions and the ethical arguments relating to pre-implantation genetic diagnosis and saviour siblings;
- appreciate the legal complexities and ethical issues surrounding surrogacy.

INTRODUCTION

This chapter is divided into three separate parts, all of which concern different aspects of assisted conception, the ethical arguments and the legal regulation.

WHAT IS ASSISTED CONCEPTION?

In 1978 Louise Brown was the world's first IVF baby to be born. Four years later, a Committee of Enquiry into Human Fertilisation and Embryology considered and recommended regulation in this new area of medicine. The Warnock Report reported in 1984, and 6 years later the Human Fertilisation and Embryology Act 1990 was passed.

NICE defines infertility, which affects 3.5 million people a year in the UK, as 'failing to get pregnant after two years of regular unprotected sex'. The Human Fertilisation and Embryology (HFE) Acts 1990 and 2008 regulate assisted conception, and any form of assisted conception carried out by clinics or research centres must be licensed by the Human Fertilisation and Embryology Authority (HFEA) which was set up by Section 5 of the Act. Part of the HFEA's role is to regulate embryo research and fertility treatment.

On-the-spot question

What do you understand by infertility? Conduct your own research by looking at the NICE website.

OWNERSHIP OF GAMETES AND ISSUES OF CONSENT

One might automatically consider that any of our gametes would belong to us even when they are separated from our body, but an issue arose in *Yearworth* (2009) as to who had legal ownership of gametes.

KEY CASE ANALYSIS: *Yearworth v North Bristol NHS Trust* [2009] EWCA 37

Facts

* Five cancer patients had stored sperm at the defendant's facilities.
* The sperm perished due to faulty storage.
* The patients sued in negligence.

Judgment

The Court of Appeal held that the hospital had stored the sperm on the patient's behalf and it was the property of the patient who had produced it. The HFE Act 2008 regulated the storage of the gametes and the patients had consented to the ways it could be used. The Trust had breached their duty of care and was liable in negligence.

Before 2005, the HFE Act 1990 stated that a gamete donor would be anonymous. Neither the couple who received the donor gametes nor the child born could ever obtain any information about the donor's identity save for matters relating to the transmission of serious medical conditions. In *R (on the application of Rose) v Secretary of State for Health* [2002] EWHC 1593 (Admin) the claimants argued that they had a right under Article 8 to a private and family life, which included the right to know their biological parent. The court accepted that Article 8 was engaged but failed to recognise the conflicting right of the donor to retain his anonymity.

It is clearly important for children to know their true identity and the law slowly changed to allow this to happen. The Human Fertilisation and Embryology Authority (Disclosure of Donor Information) Regulations 2004 now permit children over the age 18 born from gamete donation after 1 April 2005 to discover the donor's identity.

Removing gamete anonymity is important as the children born as a result can discover their true biological background and any inherited disease or condition. However, the release of donor information may also have a negative effect on a person's self-esteem and create psychological damage. They may question their role within their family unit when they learn they are not a product of their father and mother.

Consent and the use of gametes

The HFE Act 1990 Schedule 3, Paragraph 6(3) states that an embryo cannot be created unless there is consent by both parties regarding the use of the gametes for that purpose. The Schedule has proved to be very controversial.

KEY CASE ANALYSIS: *Evans v Amicus Healthcare Limited* [2004] 3 EWCA 277

Facts

- Evans was engaged to Johnston. They intended to start a family.
- They decided to freeze a fertilised embryo when Evans discovered she needed urgent medical treatment.
- A year later they separated and Johnston sought to have the embryos destroyed.

Judgment

The Court of Appeal applied Schedule 3, Paragraph 6(3) and found against Evans. As Johnston had withdrawn his consent, the embryo could not be implanted into Evans. She lost the right to become a mother. The decision was upheld by the European Court of Human Rights and the Grand Chamber *Evans v UK (App No 6339/05)* [2007]. Although Evans argued that she had a right to a private and family life (Article 8) and to become a mother, Johnston had the right not to become a father.

The court sought to balance the two parties. There is, however, an argument that the parties' interests were not equally balanced. Johnston could father children at a later stage of his life but Evans could not become a mother at a later stage.

The Act was amended in 2008 Act and Schedule 3(4A) now states that where there is a dispute regarding the use of an embryo there will be a 'cooling off' period of 1 year to allow both parties to reflect before destruction of the embryos takes place.

On-the-spot question

 Do you agree with the decision in *Evans v Amicus Healthcare Limited*? There is an argument that her right to be a mother should have outweighed his right not to be a father. Formulate your views ensuring you apply the law.

EMBRYO TESTING: PRE-IMPLANTATION GENETIC DIAGNOSIS (PGD)

Pre-implantation genetic diagnosis (PGD) is a process whereby the embryo is tested for a specific hereditary disease or a chromosomal abnormality, which takes places before an embryo is implanted into a woman by way of IVF. The Human Fertilisation and Embryology Authority and Advisory Committee on Genetic Testing's *Consultation Document on Pre-implantation Genetic Diagnosis* (2000) explains that PGD can only be used in 'certain severe life-threatening disorders'. There are over 120 conditions where PGD can be used. Small selections of the conditions are shown below.

Figure 9.1

A licence must be obtained from the HFEA. The HFE Act 2008 Schedule 2, Paragraph 1ZA(1) states that a licence under Paragraph 1 will not permit embryo testing unless its objective is:

(a) to establish the risk of chromosomal abnormality or genetic defect, which may affect a live birth;

(b) to establish the risk of chromosomal abnormality or genetic defect or mitochondrion abnormality;

(c) to establish the sex of the embryo to assess the risk of a gender-related, serious physical or mental disability or disease.

The ethics of PGD

Example

Andy and Mary want to have children but Mary is a carrier of BRCA 1, the gene that carries breast cancer. They decide to undergo genetic testing in order to determine whether an embryo carries the gene and have decided not to implant an embryo if it is found to carry that gene. She has three embryos tested. Two embryos test positive for BRCA 1 and one does not. They implant the embryo that is free from BRCA 1 and Mary subsequently gives birth to a baby girl free from the breast cancer gene.

By implanting the embryo free from the faulty gene, the two other embryos will be discarded. Arguably, by discarding the affected embryos, one is saying that embryos that are identified as having disability are not worth implanting. However, there is perhaps a more popular view that says that if one can spare a baby a life of pain and suffering, then this is preferable to the alternative. Moreover, it allows a woman to exercise her reproductive autonomy, a topic we discuss further in Chapter 10.

Saviour siblings

Since 2001 the HFEA has permitted the use of tissue typing (Human Leukocyte Antigen (HLA)) in embryos. This is a similar process to PGD and its objective is to establish not only that the embryo is disease-free but that the embryo is also an exact tissue match to its sick sibling. The embryo is implanted via IVF and when the baby is born, stem cells are taken from the baby's umbilical blood and used as lifesaving treatment for the sick sibling. The new baby is often referred to as a 'saviour sibling'.

Example

Ali and Jenna have a boy, Bill who suffers from sickle cell anaemia. They want to have another baby but it is important to them that he or she does not suffer from the same condition. They also want to be able to use the stem cells from the new baby to help treat Bill as they know that the embryos will be tested to find a perfect tissue match.

The HFE Act 2008 permits embryo testing for the purpose of 'saviour siblings'. Paragraph 1Z(d) of Schedule 2 states that where the already-living child of a person whose gametes are used to create an embryo suffers from a serious medical condition which could be treated by umbilical stem cells, bone marrow or other tissue, testing can take place to find tissue compatibility with the sick child. Paragraph 1ZA(4) specifically excludes 'other tissue', for example, organs.

'Saviour sibling' cases

In 2001, the HFEA granted a licence to the clinic treating Zain Hashmi. He was a 3-year-old boy who suffered from beta thalassaemia and needed a bone marrow transplant. The clinic applied to the HFEA to carry out PGD and tissue typing. The clinic intended to use blood from a tissue perfect match to help save Zain's life. The Hashmis had a second child who did not have beta thalassaemia but was not a tissue match and tissue typing was a way to help save Zain's life. Tissue typing found a compatible embryo and Zain was treated with umbilical stem cells once the baby was born which helped to treat him.

The law

As a result of the HFEA's decision to grant a licence to the fertility clinic treating Zain Hashmi, Josephine Quintavalle, acting on behalf of Comment on Reproductive Ethics (CORE), a pressure group committed to protecting the embryo, brought an action for judicial review.

KEY CASE ANALYSIS: *Quintavalle (Comment on Reproductive Ethics) v Human Fertilisation and Embryology Authority* [2005] UKHL 28

Facts

- It was argued that tissue typing was not permitted by the HFE Act 1990 as tissue typing did not fall within the definition of providing 'treatment services'.

Judgment

The House of Lords gave a wide interpretation to the powers of the HFEA. Activities under the Act could be carried out if they could be considered 'necessary or desirable'.

It was both necessary and desirable to obtain an embryo that was free from the condition Zain suffered from and desirable that it was tissue compatible with Zain. Tissue typing was permitted under the Act.

Are 'saviour siblings' ethically acceptable?

Table 9.1

In favour of saviour siblings	Against saviour siblings
It does not treat a baby solely as a means to an end and the baby would be loved and be a welcome addition to the family	It treats the baby as a means to an end and contrary to Kantian principles
No harm is caused to the saviour sibling who has been born free from a debilitating condition	The baby is born as 'spare parts' for the sick child of the family
The child may feel it has been born with a special role and may feel very proud and protective of its sibling	The baby is born with a specific purpose – to help its sibling. When the child gets older, it may resent the manner and reason for its birth
	If the child feels like a commodity, then the child has been harmed
	If the saviour sibling cannot save his sick sibling's life, he may feel a loss of self-esteem and that he has failed

Although Schedule 2, Paragraph 1ZA HFEA 2008 permits sex selection of embryos for the purposes of detecting 'a gender-related serious illness', it is unlawful to test an embryo to determine the sex for any reason other than for a gender-related serious illness.

There is an argument that sex selection is a woman's autonomous reproductive right. She may wish to 'balance' her family or have a particular desire for a boy or a girl. However, in some societies boys are considered far more valuable than girls for either religious or economic reasons. The risk of aborting an embryo because of its sex not only devalues and oppresses women but damages genetic diversity.

SURROGACY

Introduction

Surrogacy is the term used in the case that a woman or 'surrogate' agrees to bear a child on behalf of another woman and will hand over the baby at birth to the intended parents. The intended parents are the couple with whom the agreement has been made. According to the Children and Family Court Advisory and Support Service there were 167 babies registered in Britain to a surrogate parent in 2013 with a potentially higher number in 2014. Increasingly, surrogacy arrangements are made internationally and intended parents encounter difficulties with international law as a result.

Types of surrogacy

Partial surrogacy is where sperm is fertilised with the surrogate mother's egg, usually through artificial insemination. The surrogate therefore has a genetic link with the foetus, as does the intended father. Full or gestatory surrogacy is where both the egg and the sperm are from the intended couple and the embryo is implanted into the surrogate mother to carry to term.

Example

Bernice and Rod entered into a surrogacy agreement with Katy in the UK. Katy provides her eggs and Rod provides his gametes. This is a partial surrogacy.

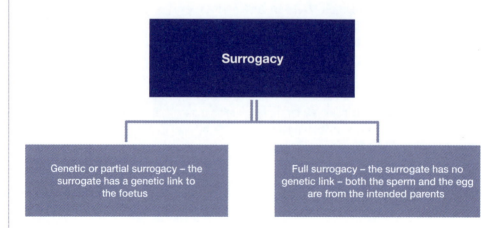

Figure 9.2

Surrogacy and the law

Section 1(2) of the Surrogacy Arrangements Act 1985 defines a 'surrogate mother' as a woman who 'carries a child in pursuance of an arrangement' with the intention of handing the baby over to the intended parents who will have parental responsibility for it. Section 36 of the Human Fertilisation and Embryology Act 1990 amended the Surrogacy Arrangements Act 1985 and Section 1B explains that a surrogacy arrangement is not enforceable against either party.

Section 2 of the Surrogacy Arrangements Act 1985 states that it is a criminal offence to be involved with the commercialisation of surrogacy. Therefore, it is not unlawful to enter into a surrogacy agreement unless it is for commercial purposes. It is lawful for a non-profit-making organisation or group to help and advise with surrogacy arrangements and Section 2A of the Human Fertilisation and Embryology Act 2008 allows the non-profit-making body to be paid a reasonable fee for facilitating or making a surrogacy arrangement. However, it remains unlawful for a person to advertise services either as a surrogate or as an intended couple.

The legal status of a surrogate child

The surrogate mother is the legal mother of the surrogate child (Section 33 HFE Act 2008) regardless of whether the surrogate mother has any genetic link to the baby she has carried.

If the surrogate is married, her husband will be the legal father of the child if he has consented to his wife acting as a surrogate. If she has a male partner, he will act as the surrogate's father if she consents. They will remain the legal parents until a parental order has transferred parentage to the intended couple. If the surrogate's husband or male partner has not consented or there is not one, then the baby will not have a legal father.

Table 9.2

Legal mother	Surrogate mother (Section 33 HFE Act 2008)
Legal father	Surrogate mother's male partner if he consents (Section 35 HFE Act 2008)
Intended parents	No legal rights until a parental order has been made

Example

Bernice and Rod entered into a surrogacy agreement with Katy in the UK. The baby has been born. What happens next?

Bernice and Rod, the intended parents, are not the legal parents. Their next step is to either apply for a parental order, which allows parenthood to be transferred from the surrogate to the intended couple, or to apply for adoption (a more complex process). In order to apply for a parental order, Section 54 of the HFE Act 2008 sets out the following criteria:

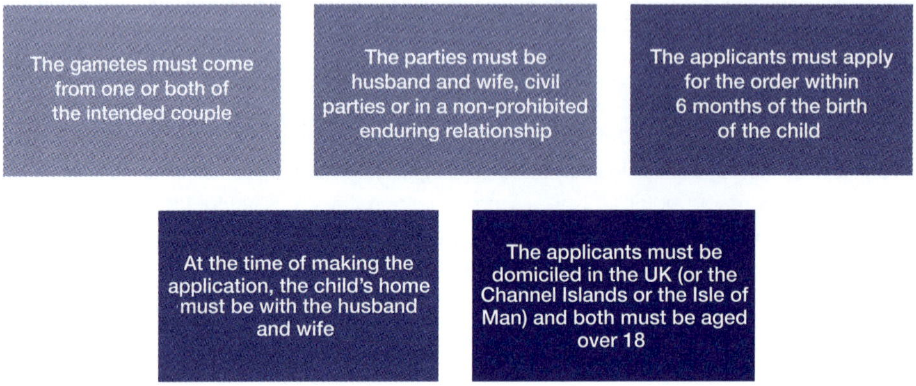

The gametes must come from one or both of the intended couple

The parties must be husband and wife, civil parties or in a non-prohibited enduring relationship

The applicants must apply for the order within 6 months of the birth of the child

At the time of making the application, the child's home must be with the husband and wife

The applicants must be domiciled in the UK (or the Channel Islands or the Isle of Man) and both must be aged over 18

Figure 9.3

The surrogate (and her male partner if appropriate) with legal responsibility must consent to the parental order. Before making the parental order under Section 54(8) the court must be satisfied that only reasonable expenses have been incurred in the surrogacy arrangements, failing which the payment will be contrary to public policy.

KEY CASE ANALYSIS: *Re C (Application by Mr and Mrs X under Section 30 of the Human Fertilisation and Embryology Act 1990)* [2002] EWHC 157 (Fam)

Facts

- The intended couple had paid the surrogate £12,000.
- The court had to determine whether these expenses had been reasonably incurred before a parental order could be made.

Judgment

Although the payment was large, it was reasonably incurred. The court approved the payment and then a parental order could be made. The court was satisfied that the couple was not attempting to buy a baby.

Similarly, in *Re X and Y (Foreign Surrogacy)* [2008] EWHC 3030 (Fam) the court agreed expenses, which although in excess of what could be described as 'reasonable', it was considered to be in the child's best interests for the parental order to be made. More recently, in *Re P-M (Parental Order: Payments to Surrogacy Agency)* [2013] EWHC 2328, which involved an international surrogacy agreement, significant payments had been made and the clinic had made a profit. Nevertheless, the court considered the criteria under Section 54 had been met and as the welfare of the surrogate twins was of paramount consideration, a parental order was made.

Surrogacy raises complex issues not only regarding potentially excessive payments but also the unenforceability of the agreement. What happens when the surrogate mother will not hand the baby to the intended parents as agreed?

Example

Bernice and Rod entered into a surrogacy agreement with Katy in the UK. The baby has been born. Katy refuses to hand the baby to the intended parents. What will happen?

The surrogate mother is the legal mother and regardless of whether the surrogacy has been full or partial, the intended parents will be unable to apply for a parental order but can apply for a residence order as an alternative. However, where the baby has been living with his or her mother, the courts will be reluctant to change the status quo. Unusually, in *Re P (Surrogacy: Residence)* [2008] 1 FLR 198 the surrogate mother was dishonest, telling the intended family that she had miscarried. Even though the baby lived with the surrogate mother for the first 18 months of his life, the court was of the view that it would be in his best interests if he were to live with the intended couple. In contrast, in *Re T (A Child) (Surrogacy: Residence)* [2011] EWHC 33 (Fam) the surrogate mother developed a close bond with the baby once born and the court held that it would be in the best interests for the child to remain with the mother.

THE ETHICS OF SURROGACY

Is harm caused to the child?

Arguably, a child born to a surrogate and then given away to intended parents may be harmed by learning that her gestational mother did not want to keep her and she may feel like a commodity. She may also feel that, out of the parents who raised her, and to whom she will be genetically related, at least one of them wanted a child to such an extent that they engaged a surrogate mother. Harm has not necessarily been caused. However, the Brazier Report recommends restricting surrogacy in case harm is in fact caused.

Exploitation

Is the surrogate exploited? By far the majority of women who act as surrogate mothers do so for altruistic reasons as there is little commercial benefit to their actions. However, reasonable expenses are still paid and these can be quite extensive. There is an argument that surrogacy exploits the poor and perpetuates the economic divide between rich and poor.

SUMMARY

- PGD and tissue typing will only be licensed in limited circumstances set down in the HFE Act.
- PGD allows an inheritable condition or chromosomal abnormality to be detected and allows the parents to choose an embryo free from a specific condition.
- 'Saviour siblings' are very uncommon but have attracted considerable ethical and legal attention.
- Where no harm is done to the saviour sibling, there is clear benefit to the sick child.
- There is no evidence that PGD or tissue typing harms a child born as a result.
- Sex selection of embryos is unlawful and ethically unacceptable.
- The law on surrogacy is complex and reform is needed.
- Particular difficulties surround what amounts to reasonable payments, the difficulties of international surrogacy and the unenforceability of the agreement.
- Surrogacy also raises difficult ethical issues and there is a potential for harm to be caused to the child.

ISSUES TO THINK ABOUT FURTHER

- Do you consider surrogacy to be ethically acceptable?
- What are the legal challenges in surrogacy? How could they be overcome?
- Spencer and Louise are unable to have children and they enter into an agreement with a surrogate, Lucy. When Lucy delivers the baby, they discover it suffers from Down's syndrome. Spencer and Louise refuse to acknowledge that they have entered into an agreement as they do not want a child with disability. Lucy did not envisage the intended parents refusing to apply for a parental order and is now looking after a baby she did not want. Consider the legal and ethical issues that arise.

FURTHER READING

D'Alton-Harrison, R. (2014) 'Mater Semper Incertus Est: Who's Your Mummy?' *Medical Law Review*, 22(3): 357–83.

Devolder, K. (2005) 'Pre –implantation HLA Typing: Having Children to Save Our Loved Ones', *Journal of Medical Ethics*, 31: 582–6.

Frith, L. (2001) 'Gamete Donation and Anonymity', *Human Reproduction*, 16(5): 818–24.

National Institute for Health and Care Excellence *https://nice.org.uk/*

For an article on surrogacy see

http://thesundaytimes.co.uk/sto/news/article1442314.ece

Chapter 10
Abortion

LEARNING OBJECTIVES

By the end of this chapter you should be able to:

- understand the provisions of the Abortion Act 1967;
- understand the legal status of a foetus;
- appreciate the complexity of the ethical arguments on abortion;
- demonstrate an understanding of both the legal and the ethical issues.

INTRODUCTION

The law on abortion in England and Wales was, historically, restrictive. The earliest piece of legislation concerning abortion was the Malicious Shooting or Stabbing Act 1803 under which it was deemed an offence to abort a foetus post quickening (around 16–18 weeks), punishable by the death penalty or transportation. The Malicious Shooting or Stabbing Act 1803 was followed by the Offences Against the Person Act 1861, and Sections 58 and 59 remain in force today. Although prosecutions under either of these sections are relatively rare, in the criminal case of *R v Catt (Sarah Louise)* [2013] EWCA 1187 a 36-year-old mother of two was sentenced to 3½ years' imprisonment (which had been reduced on appeal from 8 years) for procuring her own abortion by purchasing drugs to cause a miscarriage. The court's reference to public policy and the need for a deterrent highlights the serious criminal nature of unlawful abortions. The Infant Life (Preservation) Act 1929 was introduced alongside the Offences Against the Person Act 1861, which made it an offence punishable by life imprisonment to abort a foetus capable of being born alive. At the time the statute was written, the viability of a foetus was 28 weeks and although it is now considerably earlier, the Act remains in force today. The Abortion Act 1967, which represents the law today, was introduced in a decade of social enlightenment that included the introduction of the contraceptive pill. One of the Act's aims was to eliminate the perils of illegal and dangerous abortions. As a result of this seminal but controversial legislation, while abortion remains unlawful, the Abortion Act sets out four grounds under which a woman may legally obtain an abortion.

THE ABORTION ACT 1967

Section 1, Abortion Act 1967

Section 1, Abortion Act 1967, as amended by HFE Act 1990, states that a person will not be guilty of an offence under the Abortion Act if a pregnancy is terminated by a registered medical practitioner where two registered medical practitioners are of the opinion, in good faith, that the pregnant woman fulfils one of the statutory grounds under Section 1.

The section sets out some important facts.

- There is no 'right' to an abortion.
- A woman cannot terminate a pregnancy simply because she wishes to.
- A woman can only terminate a pregnancy if she satisfies one of the statutory grounds under Section 1.
- Two medical practitioners must be satisfied in *good faith* that the pregnant woman satisfies one of the grounds for a termination under Section 1(1)(a)–(d). However, Section 1(4) states that in the case of an emergency abortion, where the termination is immediately necessary to 'save the life or to prevent grave permanent injury to the physical or mental health of the pregnant woman' the requirement for the opinion of two medical practitioners can be dispensed with and one opinion is adequate.
- A termination of pregnancy can be carried out by someone other than a registered medical practitioner. This particular point was tested in *Royal College of Nursing of UK v DHSS* [1981] AC 800 where the wording of Section 1(1), which states that only a *'registered medical practitioner'* can conduct an abortion, could be extended to include nurses.

The principle of 'good faith'

The case of *R v Smith* [1974] 1 All ER 376 explored the meaning of 'good faith' within Section 1. Here, a young girl wanted an abortion and saw Dr Smith, who neither examined her nor explored her personal circumstances, but told her he would terminate the pregnancy if she paid him. Dr Smith was convicted of breaching the Abortion Act 1967, as he had not acted in good faith as required by Section 1. His appeal was unsuccessful and Lord Scarman made the following observations about the Abortion Act 1967:

> though it renders lawful abortions that before its enactment would have been unlawful . . . the legality of an abortion depends upon the opinion of the doctor. It has introduced the safeguard of two opinions: but, if they are formed in good faith by the time when the operation is undertaken, the abortion is lawful. Thus a great social responsibility is firmly placed by the law upon the shoulders of the medical profession.

Not only do Lord Scarman's words highlight the importance of the medical practitioner acting in good faith where consideration of abortion is concerned but the emphasis is on the medical professional's opinion rather than the pregnant woman's wish, confirming once more that a woman does not have an automatic right to an abortion.

Section 1(1)(a)–(d), Abortion Act 1967

These sections set out the circumstances in which a woman may legally have an abortion. This represents the current law in England, Scotland and Wales.

Section 1(1)(a), Abortion Act 1967

Section 1 (1)(a) permits an abortion where the pregnancy has not exceeded 24 weeks and continuing the pregnancy would involve a risk of injury to the physical or mental health of the pregnant woman or any existing children of her family greater than the risk if the pregnancy was terminated.

The termination must be carried out before the 24-week upper limit

The majority of abortions are carried out under this ground, which has often been described as a 'social' ground

The Department of Health statistics for England and Wales 2012 (published 2014) state that 91 per cent of all abortions were carried out at under 13 weeks' gestation

Figure 10.1

Example

One Friday night, Tracey, who is aged 17, goes to her local nightclub with her friends. She drinks too much and has unprotected sexual intercourse with Wayne, a boy she has just met. A few weeks later she discovers she is pregnant. She is very frightened. She has a place at sixth form college and wants to finish her studies and find a job. She becomes very distressed as she knows she is not ready to become a mother. Tracey will be able to terminate the pregnancy under Section 1(1)(a) as she is less than 24 weeks pregnant, if she can prove that there would be a risk to her mental health if the pregnancy were to continue.

Section 1(1)(b), Abortion Act 1967

This section permits an abortion where it is necessary 'to prevent grave permanent injury to the physical or mental health of the pregnant woman'. Section 1(2) relies upon the good faith of the doctor in his belief that the injury referred to in the Section exists or may exist. The injury does not therefore need to be physically present.

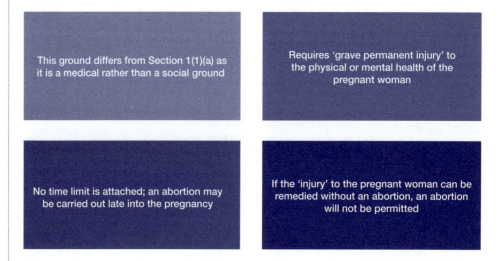

This ground differs from Section 1(1)(a) as it is a medical rather than a social ground

Requires 'grave permanent injury' to the physical or mental health of the pregnant woman

No time limit is attached; an abortion may be carried out late into the pregnancy

If the 'injury' to the pregnant woman can be remedied without an abortion, an abortion will not be permitted

Figure 10.2

Section 1(1)(c), Abortion Act 1967

This section permits an abortion where continuing with the pregnancy 'would involve risk to the life of the pregnant woman, greater than if the pregnancy were terminated'.

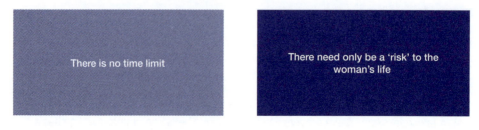

There is no time limit

There need only be a 'risk' to the woman's life

Figure 10.3

Section 1(1)(d), Abortion Act 1967

This section permits an abortion where 'there is a substantial risk that if the child were born it would suffer from such physical or mental abnormalities as to be seriously handicapped'.

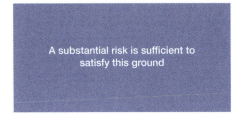

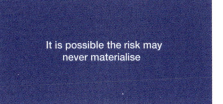

Approximately 1 per cent of abortions are carried out under this ground

Figure 10.4

Some concern has been expressed about this ground as it allows an abortion at a late stage of pregnancy where there is a risk that a child will be born with a disability. It is argued that allowing an abortion on these grounds devalues those who are disabled and perpetuates negative stereotypes of those with disability.

Example

Steph is pregnant and has been told by her midwife that she is at higher risk of carrying a Down's syndrome baby. She has an amniocentesis test at 17 weeks and the results show that there is a high probability that her baby will have Down's syndrome. Steph and her partner Martin discuss their options. Under Section 1(1)(d), Steph will be able to have an abortion as there is a substantial risk that the child, if born, will be seriously handicapped.

Section 4(1), Abortion Act 1967

This section allows a medical professional to conscientiously object to participate in any 'treatment' that involves an abortion. The statutory provision is accepted by the General Medical Council which provides guidance in the document *Personal Beliefs and Medical Practice* (2013) regarding a medical professional's conscientious objection. A doctor must act openly and respectfully towards the patient's views and refer the patient to another doctor who will be able to assist in the termination of the pregnancy.

KEY CASE ANALYSIS: *R v Salford Area Health Authority ex parte Janaway* [1988] UKHL 17

Facts

- A secretary, who was Roman Catholic and opposed to abortion, objected to typing a patient's letter relating to her abortion.

Judgment

Typing a letter did not amount to 'treatment' within the wording of the Act and she could not object in the same way that a medical professional could.

However, in the Scottish case of *Doogan v Greater Glasgow and Clyde Health Board and others* [2013] CSIH 36 the courts held that the conscientious objection under Section 4(1) extended to the entire process of treatment, not just the actual act of termination of pregnancy.

ABORTION IN OTHER JURISDICTIONS

The American case of *Roe v Wade* [1973] 410 US 113 gave a woman protected rights under the constitution to decide for herself whether or not to proceed with a pregnancy. In Northern Ireland, the law consists of the Offences Against the Person Act 1861, the Infant Life (Preservation) Act 1929 and the common law principle of necessity established in *R v Bourne* [1939] 1 KB 687. In the Republic of Ireland, a strictly Catholic country, abortion is now permitted in limited circumstances. By virtue of The Protection of Life During Pregnancy Act 2013, effective from January 2014, terminations of pregnancy are permitted in limited circumstances. Abortions will be permitted where there is a real and substantial risk to the woman's life from a physical illness, which can only be prevented by the termination of pregnancy whether immediate or not and where there is a real and substantial risk of the woman's suicide. Due to the restrictive nature of the law in both Northern Ireland and the Republic of Ireland, many women travel to England and Wales to terminate their pregnancy.

PATIENTS WHO LACK CAPACITY

Where a patient who lacks capacity (as defined by the Mental Capacity Act 2005) is pregnant, it could be a matter of clinical judgment as to whether the pregnant woman's best interests are served by terminating the pregnancy.

KEY CASE ANALYSIS: *Re SS (An Adult: Medical Treatment)* [2002] 1 FLR 445

Facts

- S was schizophrenic, a mother of four children, 24 weeks pregnant and wished to have an abortion.

Judgment

The court held that, on balance, it would not be in her best interests to have an abortion and that the best option would be for S to give birth and then have the baby removed.

In contrast, in *Re SB (A Patient) (Capacity to Consent to Termination)* [2013] EWHC 1417 (COP), a 37-year-old woman who suffered from bipolar disorder and was nearly 24 weeks pregnant was able to have an abortion. Both women suffered from illnesses under the Mental Health Act 1983 but SB was able to clearly articulate the reasons why she wished to have an abortion.

Example

Martha suffers from schizophrenia and has been sectioned under the Mental Health Act 1983. She discovers she is 20 weeks pregnant and does not feel that she can manage to bring up a baby given her current condition. Although there are decisions that she does not have capacity to make she is very certain that she does not wish to have a baby. In these circumstances, it is likely that the court will agree that it is not in her best interests for the pregnancy to continue.

THE LEGAL STATUS OF A FOETUS

A foetus only gains legal status once it is delivered from its mother. A foetus has no rights until it is born. In *Attorney-General's Reference (No 3 of 1994)* [1997] 3 All ER 936, Lord

Mustill said that 'the foetus does not have the attributes which make it a "person"; it must be an adjunct of the mother'.

In *Paton v British Pregnancy Advisory Service* [1978] 2 All ER 98, the court held that 'The foetus cannot, in English law, in my view, have any right of its own at least until it is born and has a separate existence from the mother.' Mr Paton took his case to the European Courts (*Paton v UK* [1981] 3 EHRR 408), unsuccessfully arguing that as the father of the unborn child he could protect the foetus's life under Article 2 (the right to life). Moreover, he also argued that his own right to respect for family life was violated under Article 8. This judgment confirms that it is the woman's sole decision whether or not to proceed with or terminate a pregnancy. The principle was also confirmed in *St George's Healthcare Trust v S* [1998] 3 All ER 673, where the Court of Appeal confirmed that a competent patient could refuse medical treatment even if such refusal would lead to the unborn child's death.

Example

Mark and Stacey are expecting their first child. Stacey feels that she is not ready to be a mother; she is absorbed in her career and wishes to have an abortion. Mark is distressed by her decision and says that the baby has rights and she should not be able to abort the foetus. He takes legal advice and is told that, following the decision of *Paton v British Pregnancy Advisory Service* [1978], the foetus does not have any rights until it is born. Consequently, Stacey can, if she fulfills one of the grounds under Section 1(1)(a)–(d), terminate the pregnancy.

ABORTION AND ETHICS

Introduction

Without doubt, abortion is a controversial topic that tends to raise an emotional response. When you read the following section, try to remain neutral and consider the arguments without emotional attachment. There is nothing wrong with having an opinion on the ethics of abortion, provided it is supported by analysis, debate and a thorough understanding. There are generally one of two positions a person may take. One view is that at any stage abortion is abhorrent and, once conception has taken place, the foetus should be regarded as a person and cannot be aborted. The other view is that it is the woman's autonomous decision what she decides to do with her body. We shall see that there is also a middle ground. We begin the discussion with a focus on the moral status of the foetus.

The foetus at conception

There is a belief that the foetus is a person from conception, the time at which the sperm enters the egg. Although this is often considered to be a religious view, Finnis (1973) argues that when the sperm unites with the egg it forms a 'unique genetic constitution' and a new individual is created with its own identity. Hence, Finnis maintains that there is a fixed point at which life begins and, from that point onwards, abortion is not permissible.

Can a foetus be considered a person?

Mary A. Warren maintains that a foetus cannot be treated as a person simply because it has the potential to be one. Simply because a foetus can develop into a person does not mean that it is human before the point at which it is born. Moreover, even if it can be established that the foetus does have some right to life, it cannot outweigh the pregnant woman's self-determination. She argues that there are characteristics that can identify what amounts to a person and, should these not be present, the foetus cannot be a human in the moral sense. Some of the characteristics that Mary Warren refers to are set out below.

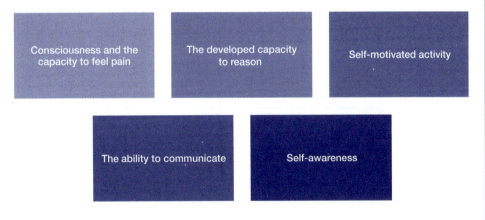

Figure 10.5

Approaches by academics differ. Marquis (1989) takes a pro-life approach arguing that abortion 'is in the same moral category as killing an innocent adult human being'. He accepts that there are limited exceptions, for example, where pregnancy results from rape. But to kill a foetus in other circumstances deprives it of the valuable future it would have had. In contrast, Savulescu (2002) argues that, although a foetus might be deprived of its future if aborted, simply preventing the future is not the same as killing, as an abortion before 20 weeks is 'no different from discarding a sperm and an egg, or an embryo, or a skin cell'.

If while reading this you are considering that it may be ethically acceptable to abort a foetus, you may also be considering the point at which it is acceptable compared to when it no longer remains ethically acceptable. If you were to accept that a foetus is a person at conception then abortion is never acceptable. If you reject this theory then consider at what point in a baby's gestation abortion is acceptable. In order to help, consider the gradualist view which invites you to consider the physical development of the foetus. Mary Warnock addresses this view by explaining that the more the foetus develops, the more emotionally connected we feel towards it and the more protective we become. At 3 months pregnancy may not be physically apparent and some women may find it difficult to relate to the pregnancy in quite the same terms as a woman who is 7 or 8 months pregnant and who is likely to be more protective and nurturing towards her future baby. The greater the development, the more difficult it is to terminate its life. Gradualists argue that the more the foetus has developed, the greater respect the foetus should be owed. Moreover, the greater respect that is given to the foetus, the more difficult it is to ethically justify an abortion. So far, we have considered the rights of the foetus. We now turn to consider the pregnant woman.

On-the-spot question

To what extent do you agree with these moral arguments concerning the status of a foetus? Do you agree that a foetus is a person upon conception? If you do not agree with this theory, is there a stage in gestation when you consider abortion to no longer be ethically acceptable? How would you support your decision?

The pregnant woman

Arguably, a pregnant woman has the right to decide for herself whether a pregnancy should continue. It was exactly this point that was raised before the European Court of Human Rights. In *Tysiac v Poland* [2007] 22 BHRC 155 a Polish woman was denied the abortion that she sought from the state on medical grounds. She had been advised that her eyesight would deteriorate if her pregnancy continued. She eventually obtained permission to have an abortion but the hospital refused to carry it out. Since she was unable to obtain an abortion, she had no alternative but to give birth with considerably impaired vision. She argued that the government had failed to respect her Article 8 right (to a private and family life). The European Court of Human Rights accepted that her rights had been violated and she received compensation. Although the ECHR was not saying that every woman has a right to an abortion under the Convention, it is highly suggestive of exactly this point.

Mary Ann Warren advocates the right of the pregnant woman over that of the foetus and the prevailing principle is vividly demonstrated in 'The violinist analogy'. Written by Judith Jarvis Thomson, *A Defense of Abortion* was published in 1971 and remains one of the most applauded arguments on abortion. Thomson's creates the analogy of a famous violinist who has been 'attached' to you overnight.

> You wake up in the morning and find yourself back-to-back in bed with an unconscious violinist. A famous, unconscious violinist. He has been found to have a fatal kidney ailment, and the Society of Music Lovers has canvassed all the available medical records and found that you alone have the right blood type to help. They have therefore kidnapped you, and last night the violinist's circulatory system was plugged into yours, so that your kidneys can be used to extract poisons from his blood as well as your own.

You are told that you may 'unplug' yourself from him but he will die. If you remain hooked up to him, it will be for a period of 9 months. You may chose to remain plugged to the violinist but you might also decide that you are not obliged to remain attached to a life form dependent upon you should you not wish to do so. Should you choose to unplug yourself, you are simply exercising your right to self-determination and bodily integrity. If you were to unplug yourself from the violinist, he would die. Arguably, there is a difference between this analogy and abortion as terminating a pregnancy may be more akin to intentionally killing the foetus as opposed to letting the violinist die.

Thomson continues:

> people-seeds drift about in the air like pollen, and if you open your windows, one may drift in and take root in your carpets and your upholstery. You don't want children, so you fix up your windows with fine mesh screens, the very best you can buy. As can happen, however, and on very, very rare occasions does happen, one of the screens is defective; and a seed drifts in and takes root . . . Someone may argue that you are responsible for its rooting, that it does have a right to your house because after all you could have lived out your life with bare floors and furniture, or with sealed windows and doors.

Here, she appears to draw on the analogy of *mesh screens* as symbolising contraception and a defective mesh screen as failed contraception. She argues that, where a woman uses contraception, this is an indication that she wishes not be become pregnant. If she takes the necessary precaution and still falls pregnant, it would be an unwanted pregnancy and the pregnant woman is justified in seeking an abortion. In this way, it appears relatively straightforward to justify a woman's self-determination and her rights over that of the foetus. Thomson then demonstrates the lack of self-determination for the pregnant woman in an analogy to a child growing inside a tiny house where the room does not get bigger.

Suppose you find yourself trapped in a tiny house with a growing child. I mean a very tiny house, and a rapidly growing child – you are already up against the wall of the house and in a few minutes you'll be crushed to death. The child on the other hand won't be crushed to death; if nothing is done to stop him from growing he'll be hurt, but in the end he'll simply burst open the house and walk out a free man. Now I could well understand it if a bystander were to say, 'There's nothing we can do for you. We cannot choose between your life and his, we cannot be the ones to decide who is to live, we cannot intervene.'

Here, there is mention of a third party. One might surmise that this is the medical professional who is not in a position to help the pregnant woman. This confirms that a pregnant woman does not have a right to an abortion per se, in which case the woman lacks self-determination. However, as Thomson says, the foetus does not have equal ownership of the house, but just rents it, and concludes by stating that the woman's right to bodily integrity and self-determination overrides any right a foetus may have.

On-the-spot question

? Try and summarise the main arguments in 'The violinist's analogy'. To what extent do you consider that this is supportive of the self-determination of a pregnant woman? Tip: in order to fully address this question, you will need to read the article (see below for the reference).

SUMMARY

- The law in England, Scotland and Wales is governed by the Abortion Act 1967. Where a pregnant woman can satisfy one of the four grounds in Section 1(1) of the Abortion Act 1967, an abortion may be permitted.
- The Abortion Act is not in force in Northern Ireland or the Republic of Ireland.
- The foetus has no legal rights in law.
- The ethics of abortion require a balancing act between the moral status of the foetus and the rights of the pregnant woman.
- There is considerable debate as to whether a foetus is a person at conception or at which point it may be ethically permissible to terminate a pregnancy. These arguments focus on the moral status of the foetus.
- Such debates neglect the pregnant woman's right to self-determination and her rights over the foetus.

ISSUES TO THINK ABOUT FURTHER

- Having demonstrated an understanding of the grounds under which an abortion is permitted, do you consider that the law is too restrictive or too liberally drafted?
- It has often been said that the law simply permits abortion on demand. Do you agree with this view?
- Section 1(1)(d) allows an abortion where there is a serious risk that if the baby were to be born it would be seriously handicapped. Do you agree that aborting a disabled foetus devalues disabled lives and is tantamount to saying that disabled lives are not worth living? Having considered the ethical arguments relating to abortion, have your initial views in relation to abortion altered at all?

FURTHER READING

Finnis, J. (1973) 'The Rights and Wrongs of Abortion', *Philosophy and Public Affairs*, 2: 117–45.

MacKenzie, C. (1992) 'Abortion and Embodiment', *Australasian Journal of Philosophy*, 70(2): 136–55.

Marquis, D. (1989) 'Why Abortion is Immoral', *Journal of Philosophy*, 86(4): 183–202.

Savulescu, J. (2002) 'Abortion, Embryo, Destruction and the Future of Value Argument', *Journal of Medical Ethics*, 28: 133–5.

Thomson, J. (1971) 'A Defense of Abortion', *Philosophy and Public Affairs*, Autumn, 47–66.

Warren, M.A. (1973) 'On the Moral and Legal Status of Abortion', *The Monist*, 1: 43–61.

Chapter 11
Organ donation

LEARNING OBJECTIVES

By the end of this chapter you should be able to:

- consider whether the body is property;
- understand the background to the Human Tissue Act 2004;
- appreciate the basic provisions of the Human Tissue Act 2004;
- understand the issues surrounding organ donation;
- demonstrate an appreciation of ways to maximise organ donation.

DO WE OWN OUR BODY?

The extent to which the body can be considered 'property' is still largely unresolved in law. Traditionally, the view was that the body was not property and could not be stolen. However, in the case below an exception of the use of 'work and skill' (*Doodeward and Spence* [1908] 6 CLR 406) was applied.

KEY CASE ANALYSIS: *R v Kelly* [1998] 3 All ER 741

Facts

- The defendant was an artist and had permission to draw body parts held at the Royal College of Surgeons.
- Over a period of several months, he arranged to steal a number of body parts.
- He made casts of the body parts and then exhibited them.
- He appealed against his conviction for theft arguing that body parts were not property.

Held

- As the body parts had been subject to skill, due to their artistic application, they could amount to property for the purposes of the Theft Act 1968 and were capable of being stolen.
- The court also suggested that retrieved organs could possibly amount to property stating that 'the common law does not stand still. It may be that if, on some future occasion, the question arises, the courts will hold that human body parts are capable of being property for the purposes of Section 4, even without the acquisition of different attributes, if they have a use or significance beyond their mere existence. This may be so if, for example, they are intended for use in an organ transplant operation, for the extraction of DNA or, for that matter, as an exhibit in a trial.'

In contrast, in the case of *Dobson v North Tyneside Health authority* [1996] 4 All ER the court held there was no ownership of a corpse and the next of kin of the deceased could not recover his brain when it had been removed for autopsy, treated and stored. The more recent case below had to consider whether sperm which was negligently stored by the hospital amounted to 'property' for the purposes of the claimant's action in bailment.

KEY CASE ANALYSIS: *Yearworth v North Bristol NHS Trust* [2009] EWCA 37

Facts

- Five men were diagnosed with cancer.
- They were advised to produce samples of sperm for storage purposes in case chemotherapy damaged their fertility.
- The sperm had to be stored in liquid nitrogen which fell below the required level and the sperm perished.
- The men sued the hospital as a claim in personal injury could not be brought.
- Who owned the sperm? Was it the hospital who had failed to store it appropriately or the claimants?

Held

- The previous common law approach in *Doodeward v Spence* was rejected.
- The hospital breached its duty of care in the storage of the sperm and was negligent.

- The sperm was the property of the men as they had produced it themselves for their own future benefit.
- They had a right to determine how the sperm should be used and could withdraw their consent to its use.
- Although the hospital (as a licence holder under the Human Fertilisation and Embryology Authority) also had duties concerning the sperm, the men had ultimate rights over its usage and, accordingly, owned the property.

Although this case was neatly resolved, the issue as to ownership of a body or body parts remains unclear.

THE BACKGROUND TO THE HUMAN TISSUE ACT 2004

The Kennedy Inquiry 1998 was set up to investigate the deaths of a number of babies who had died undergoing heart surgery at the Bristol Royal Infirmary during the late 1980s and 1990s. Most of the Inquiry's findings are beyond the scope of this chapter and indeed this book.

It transpired that a significant number of the children's organs had been retained at both the Bristol Royal Infirmary and the Alder Hey Children's Hospital in Liverpool without the parents' consent. As investigations into organ retention widened, it was discovered that many organs from children who had died had been retained by pathologists over a number of years. Retention of these organs was for the purposes of research, education or furtherance of knowledge, and the pathologists did not consider that their failure to gain the parents' consent was improper. The pathologists believed that they were acting sympathetically by not exposing the parents to any further distress.

KEY CASE ANALYSIS: *A and B v Leeds Teaching Hospitals NHS Trust and another* **[2004] EWHC 644 (QB)**

Facts

- Three claimants in a group action claimed damages for psychiatric injury from a number of hospitals.
- The claimants were parents of children whose organs had been removed at post mortem without parental consent.

- They claimed damages for psychiatric injury, wrongful interference, a breach of duty of care and breach of the Human Rights Act 1998.

Held

- Removal of the organs fell within the Human Tissue Act 1961. Where the organs had been lawfully removed for the purposes of post mortem, there was no right of burial and no right of possession.
- A doctor could owe parents a duty of care to explain the reasons for removal of the deceased's organs.
- One of the claims for psychiatric injury succeeded.

The Human Tissue Act 2004

Largely as a result of the findings of the inquiry the Human Tissue Act 2004 was enacted in order 'to provide a consistent legislative framework relating to the whole body donation and the taking, storage and use of human organs and tissue' (The Human Tissue Act 2004).

The Act also hoped to restore public confidence in relation to the removal of organs, an essential element as far as organ donation is concerned. The issue of consent underpins the Act which states that 'It will make consent the fundamental principle underpinning the lawful storage and use of human bodies, body parts, organs and tissue and the removal of material from bodies of deceased persons.'

On-the-spot question

 Explain clearly the reasons why the Human Tissue Act was enacted.

Table 11.1

Section 1	Requires that 'appropriate consent' is obtained before removal, storage and use of 'relevant material' from a cadaver (deceased person) or storage and removal of relevant material from a person who is living
Section 53	Defines relevant material by *including* tissue and material which includes cells, but *excluding* gametes, embryos, hair or nails from a living person. Organs such as kidneys are included in this definition
Sections 2 and 3	The sections define consent. Express consent is required and must be relevant to the specific purpose for which it is granted. The Human Tissue Authority Code of Practice 2 (March 2013) states that 'for consent to be valid it must be given voluntarily by an appropriately informed person who has the capacity to agree to the activity in question'
Section 5(1)	It is a now a criminal offence to remove organs or tissue without appropriate consent
Section 5(3)	There is a defence of reasonable belief if the person who removed organs or tissue without consent reasonably believed that consent had been obtained or was not required by statute

THE DEFINITION OF DEATH IN THE UK

For the purposes of organ transplantation, it is important to be able to precisely determine when a patient dies. In the UK there is no statutory definition of death although the accepted definition is now brain stem death.

Historically, death was defined as cardio pulmonary failure (when the heart and lungs had ceased to function). This definition was logical and widely accepted. However, significant advancements in medical technology, in particular assisted ventilation, meant that the body could be maintained artificially and the traditionally accepted definition of death ceased to have any clear meaning. In 1954 the first kidney transplant was successfully performed in Boston, USA and in 1967 the first heart transplant was carried out in South Africa. Technology was advancing and the traditional definition of death no longer seemed applicable.

Although death had been defined as brain stem death earlier in the USA, it was not until 1995 that a document in the *Journal of the Royal College of Physicians* entitled 'Criteria for the Diagnosis of Brain Death' accepted brain stem death as the definition of death, defining it as 'irreversible loss of the capacity for consciousness, combined with irreversible loss of the capacity to breathe'.

The difficulty of determining the moment of death when a patient is on a life support system is illustrated in *R v Malcherek* [1981] 2 All ER 422 where Lord Lane CJ (at 426) observed:

> There is, it seems a body of opinion in the medical profession that there is only one true test of death and that is the irreversible death of the brain stem, which controls the back of the basic functions of the body such as breathing. When that occurs it is said that the body has died, even though by mechanical means the lungs are being caused to operate and some circulation of blood is taking place.

The judicial acceptance of brain stem death as the definition of death was also illustrated in the later seminal case of *Airedale NHS Trust v Bland* [1993] AC 789 where Lord Keith observed that in 'the eyes of the medical world and of the law, a person is not clinically dead so long as the brain stem retains its function'.

On-the-spot question

 Do you accept brain stem death as an acceptable definition of death?

ORGAN DONATION IN THE UK

There are insufficient available organs to meet the demand of those patients waiting for organ transplantations. The following table illustrates the number of organ transplants which took place during the period April 2011–March 2012 (a total of 3,960 organ transplantations.

Table 11.2

Heart, lung, liver or combination heart/lung/liver lifesaving operations	1,107
Kidney or pancreas life-improving operations	2,846
Sight restoration operations (corneal transplant)	3,521
Living donor transplants	1,009
Total number of people on the NHS Organ Donor Register as at March 2012	18,693,549

Source: NHS Blood and Transplant

Despite nearly 4,000 organ transplants being carried out, there were still 7,403 patients waiting for organs to become available for transplantation (March 2013). Statistics show that three patients a day die (source: NHS Blood and Transplant) while waiting for organs to become available.

Example

Stan dies in hospital. He has indicated that he wishes to donate his organs on his death. Who receives his organs?

The most important factors are compatibility (such as blood type). The size and age of the organ is also relevant. It is unlikely that Stan's organs will be suitable for a child. If a child is waiting for a heart/kidney/liver or lung transplant the reality is that another child will have to die before organs can be donated. The amount of time a person has been waiting is also relevant but ability to pay, valuable employment or having dependent children are not relevant factors.

Thus far, we have established that there are insufficient organs to meet the demand of those on the NHS Organ Donor Transplant waiting list and that some patients will invariably die while waiting for an organ that may never materialise. By far the majority of organs are donated after a person's death (cadaveric organs) but there are also some live organ donations.

Live organ donations

In the period shown in the table above, 1,009 kidneys were donated during the donor's lifetime. This amounts to one-third of all kidneys transplanted. Some of these donations are purely altruistic, whereas some are paired donations (usually between couples, each of whom have a kidney to donate but are not compatible with the person they wish to donate to but the other person in the couple is compatible) or pooled donations (where two or more pairs of donors and recipients are involved in a kidney swap).

Many people regularly donate blood as a simple, accessible and largely non-intrusive act which benefits others. Altruistic acts can also extend to the donation of bone marrow but the issue of donation of a non-regenerative organ raises different and complex issues. A person is unable to consent to donate their heart as this will result in their certain death (even where a parent wishes to donate their heart to save their child's life) but one can consent to donating their kidney and/or part of their liver during their lifetime. A person can live a perfectly normal life with one kidney and the liver will effectively regenerate the donated part.

Live organ donations and the law

Live organ donation is governed by both the common law and statute. Section1 of the Human Tissue Act 2004 sets out the framework for the storage and use of material from a human body. Section 1(1)(d) states that appropriate consent is required for the storage or use of relevant material, which can include transplantation (Schedule 1, Part 1).

The competent adult

Example

Alex wishes to donate her kidney to her cousin Adam. Tests show that she is a compatible match to Adam. Alex is over 18 years of age and has capacity to consent. The law permits Alex to donate 'relevant material' with her express written consent. She must provide her consent voluntarily and she must be adequately informed of the risks of the procedure.

The incompetent adult

A person who lacks capacity cannot consent to organ donation. An incompetent person may still donate an organ if the court considers it to be in their best interests.

KEY CASE ANALYSIS: *Re Y* [1997] 12 FCR 172

Facts

- Y lacked capacity to consent to donate bone marrow to her sister.
- There was no therapeutic value to Y but donating her bone marrow could save her sister's life.

Held

- Connell J held that it would be in Y's interests to donate bone marrow as best interests were widely defined.
- Best interests were not limited to clinical consideration but included psychological and emotional aspects.
- If Y donated bone marrow, her sister would probably recover and Y's mother would be able to continue visiting Y on a regular basis.
- Y's status quo would remain the same.

Re Y (heard before The Human Tissue Act 2004 (Persons who Lack Capacity to Consent and Transplants) Regulations 2006) considered bone marrow (regenerative) but the issue would become more complex where the question concerned harvesting a non-regenerative organ such as a kidney from a patient who lacked capacity to consent. The US case of *Strunk v Strunk* [1969] 445 SW 2d 145 allowed a kidney transplant from a non-competent person to his brother on the basis that best interest could be widely defined.

The child as organ donor

Under the Human Tissue Act, a child is defined as a person less than 18 years of age. The Human Tissue Authority Code of Practice A 2013 states that organ donations from children would only be permitted in 'extremely rare circumstances' and any donation would have to be approved by the court. The potential donor's interests will be the paramount consideration, rather than the potential recipient. The Code (A9) states

> As with cases involving adults lacking capacity, this is because the procedure is not, on the face of it, therapeutic and obviously in the best interests of the prospective donor child. The court will have to determine, based on the evidence, whether it is in fact in the best interests of the prospective donor child. This test is not limited to medical interests, and should take account of potential emotional, psychological and social benefits and risks.

It is also worth noting Lord Donaldson's obiter statement in *Re W (A Minor)* [1992] 3 WLR 758, where he opined that a competent minor's ability to consent to medical treatment under the Family Law (Reform) Act 1969 would be very unlikely to extend to organ donation.

The sale of live organs – the law

Section 32 of the Human Tissue Act 2004 prohibits the sale of live organs. Section 32(1) states that a person commits a criminal offence if he 'gives or receives a reward for the supply of, or for an offer to supply, any controlled material' or is involved in the commercialisation of the supply of live organs.

Although the sale of live organs is unlawful, a black market in the trade of organs thrives. The rich pay large sums of money to obtain a compatible organ without lengthy periods of time spent on the Organ Donor Transplant waiting list with their health deteriorating further. The poor are selling their organs, and see no other option to achieve access to finance, and the middle men make a healthy profit, depriving the poor of the true value of their organ. The distribution of available organs should be based on need not wealth.

THE SALE OF LIVE ORGANS: THE ETHICS

Example

Nikita has no employment, lives in a slum dwelling which is threatened with demolition, has little access to free healthcare or state benefit. She has a seriously ill child who she could help if she could buy medicine. Nikita considers selling her kidney. For her, the benefits of selling her kidney outweigh any potential burden. Her priority is her sick child who, with the money she will earn from the sale of her kidney, will be better cared for for the foreseeable future. This is Nikita's only way of improving her and her child's lifestyle.

Is Nikita's decision ethically acceptable? The ethical arguments in favour of Nikita selling her organ are briefly set out below.

- From a utilitarian perspective, the sale of organs will increase the number of available organs thereby improving the recipient's life as well as her own.
- Her autonomous wish to sell a kidney should be respected.
- Selling her organs will improve her and her child's quality of life and this is beneficial.

In contrast, there is a compelling view that the sale of live organs is ethically unacceptable.

- It treats a person as a commodity and is contrary to deontological principles that a person should not be used solely as a means to an end.
- It is questionable whether Nikita's consent can provide true and informed consent when she has no realistic alternative.
- Nikita is being exploited (but arguably she would be less exploited if she sold an organ as her choices would be widened).

MAXIMISING ORGAN DONATION

The current system in the UK: Opt-in or express consent

Similar to joining the gym or a club, if a person wishes to become an organ donor in the UK, they must register their intention by signing the Organ Donor Register either online or in traditional paper form. There are also other ways of indicating willingness to donate organs on death and these currently include the new style UK driving licence or by way of schemes such as the Boots Advantage Card (a loyalty card).

Hence, the current method adopted in the UK is referred to as opt-in or express consent since it is necessary to take a positive step to donate organs on death by expressly indicating an intention to do so.

If a person has not expressed a wish to donate his organs on his death, it is permissible for a relative to consent to organ donation on the deceased's behalf. However, relatives' refusal (which has risen to over 40 per cent (Bird and Harris, 2010)) is one of the main reasons why transplantation teams miss the opportunity of vital organs for transplantation.

If the deceased consented to the donation of his organs during his lifetime, the Human Tissue Authority's Code of Practice, March 2013 (Clause 99) states that the matter should be discussed sensitively with the relatives of the deceased but the relatives cannot overrule the deceased's wishes to donate organs. The Code of Practice explains that despite the fact that there is no family veto, each case should be considered on its merits.

Opt-out or presumed consent

One way of potentially increasing the rates of organ donation in the UK is to introduce presumed consent or opt-out. Presumed consent would be expensive to introduce. A significant investment in educating the population would be needed. If there were more organ donors, a greater number of kidney transplantations (for example) could be conducted, freeing kidney patients from time-consuming and costly dialysis and allowing them to return home, to lead healthier lives, returning to work and contributing to family life. The cost in promoting organ donation could well result in a significantly lower burden on the NHS which is caring for patients on the Organ Donor waiting list.

There is little doubt that countries such as Belgium and Finland who have introduced presumed consent have higher organ donation rates, although Austria did not witness such an increase in organ donors. However, Spain has a significant 33.8 organ donors per million population. Although the introduction of presumed consent in Spain may account for some of the increased donation rates, credit must also be given for a sophisticated organ transplantation infrastructure which has been able to maximise organ donation. Some countries that originally opted for presumed consent have, in fact, reversed their policy following a sense of distrust between the medical professional and the patient.

In December 2013, the Welsh Assembly passed the Human (Transplantation) Act Wales 2013, which introduces a soft opt-out system for organ donation in Wales. The Act permits an assumption of consent to removal of the deceased's organs and tissues unless he or she objected to organ donation during their lifetime and opted out. The next of kin will be involved in the decision-making process. It is hoped that organ donation rates will increase by 25–30 per cent as a result of the Act.

The British Medical Association (BMA) is in favour of presumed consent, which presumes that a person is content to donate their organs upon their death unless they specifically opt out expressing their unwillingness to donate.

However, in 2008 the Organ Donation Taskforce reported on the potential drawbacks of introducing presumed consent in the UK. The report recommended that presumed consent should not be introduced for the following reasons:

1   Presuming a person's consent would undermine the idea of organ donation being a gift.
2   Presumed consent would have an adverse effect on trust between health professionals and the government.
3   The focus should be on improving the infrastructure of organ donation systems.
4   There should be more attention given to improving public awareness of the importance of organ donation.
5   There was no clear evidence that presumed consent would improve organ donation rates.

On-the-spot question

 What do you understand by presumed consent? Do you believe that it would be an effective way of maximising organ donation? Carefully explain your views.

Mandated choice

Mandated choice ensures that every person decides what will happen to their organs on their death. This would avoid relying on the deceased's relatives to make a decision in circumstances where the deceased had not considered organ donation. This could be done either through tax returns or through the state benefit system.

Compulsory removal of organs from the deceased

A more extreme measure, but one that would ensure a plentiful supply of organs would be if organs were automatically removed from the deceased. As John Harris explains (Harris, 2002), since we have no interests in our organs after our death and removal of our organs would not harm us, they should be removed even without our express consent. While there may be considerable advantage in terms of available organs for donation, it would fail to respect religious or cultural views and the deceased's express wishes.

Education

One method of creating greater awareness of organ donation could be to introduce the issue into Personal, Health and Social Education as part of the national curriculum in schools. This would be an effective way of introducing the subject to young adults and a way of allowing the subject into family life.

Campaigns

Campaigns are an alternative method of increasing awareness of the need for organ donors and a recent campaign by the ITV network 'From the Heart' aired in February 2013, motivated 48,000 people in a single day to pledge their organs to help others on their death. While this may sound significant, and indeed it is, we must recognise that it is the result of a single campaign and, for the most part, people are apathetic about the subject of organ donation.

Incentives for organ donation

Organ donation is considered to be an altruistic act, a charitable act of great kindness and therefore, arguably, it would not be ethically acceptable to financially reward the donor for her act of compassion and kindness.

To this end, the Nuffield Council on Bioethics recommended in October 2011 that funeral expenses could be paid for the benefit of the deceased where the deceased had indicated a willingness to donate organs on her death and she died in circumstances that meant she was able to do so. Hence the payment is seen as a form of gratitude, does not amount to commercialisation and is not open to accusations of being contrary to deontological principles by treating people solely as a means to an end. However, it is arguable that a balance can be achieved between paying someone for donating an organ on their death (financially rewarding them) and creating a financial incentive to donate. Other ways of creating incentives for people to donate organs on their death could include providing tax breaks or giving those who indicate their willingness to donate a higher priority on the organ transplant waiting list.

On-the-spot question

 Discuss different methods of increasing organ donation. To what extent do you consider these to be ethically acceptable?

SUMMARY

- The law remains unclear as to ownership of a body or body parts.
- The Human Tissue Act 2004 was introduced to address the organ retention scandal and introduced requirement of consent where the removal of human organs and tissues was concerned.
- There is a lack of available organs for transplantation. Three patients die every day waiting for organs for transplantation.
- The UK adopts an opt-in or express consent system for organ donation purposes.
- The main alternatives to opt-in are opt-out (presumed consent), mandated choice or removal of organs on death regardless of the deceased's wishes (an extreme measure).
- There are a number of other ways in which organ donation could be maximised.
- The Human (Transplantation) Act Wales 2013 introduces presumed consent in Wales.

ISSUES TO THINK ABOUT FURTHER

- Presumed consent for organ donation will be introduced in Wales in 2015. Having read the Act, http://legislation.gov.uk/anaw/2013/5/pdfs/anaw_20130005_en.pdf, together with other material, to what extent do you consider that presumed consent will increase the number of organ donors in Wales. If it is successful, should the rest of the UK follow suit?
- To what extent do you consider that altruism and voluntariness are removed from the potential organ donor with the introduction of presumed consent?

FURTHER READING

To gain an understanding of organ donation read the website, reports and statistics at NHS Blood and Transplant www.nhsbt.nhs.uk/

Bird, S. and Harris, J. (2010) 'Time to Move to Presumed Consent for Organ Donation', *British Medical Journal*, 340: 2188.

BMA Report (February 2012) 'Building on Progress; Where Next for Organ Donation in the UK'.

Harris, J. (2002) 'Law and Regulation of Retained Organs: The Ethical Issues', *Legal Studies*, 22(4): 527–49.

Price, D. (2005) 'The Human Tissue Act 2004', *Modern Law Review* , 68: 798–821.

Ravitsky, V. (2013) 'Incentives for Post-mortem Organ Donation: Ethical and Cultural Considerations', *Journal of Medical Ethics*, 39: 380–1.

Chapter 12
End of life decisions (1): Assisted suicide and euthanasia

LEARNING OBJECTIVES

By the end of this chapter you should be able to:

- understand the difference between euthanasia and assisted suicide;
- appreciate the statutory definition of assisted suicide;
- demonstrate an understanding of the common law decisions;
- understand the ethical arguments.

INTRODUCTION

Assisted suicide and euthanasia are highly topical and controversial areas of bioethics that raise fundamental questions about our society. Should a person's desire to end their life at a time of their choosing outweigh the protection of society and the vulnerable?

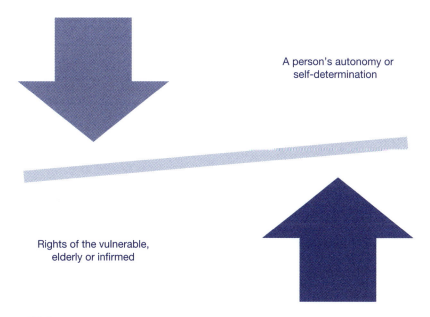

A person's autonomy or self-determination

Rights of the vulnerable, elderly or infirmed

Figure 12.1

We begin our discussion by distinguishing between euthanasia and assisted suicide.

Table 12.1

Assisted suicide	Euthanasia
Assistance is given to the person in order that they can end their life themselves The intention is to cause the person's death	Medication is given to a person at their request with the intention of hastening that person's death
	'Euthanasia involves not merely assisting another to commit suicide, but actually bringing about the death of another'. *R (on the application of Nicklinson) and Lamb v MOJ and DPP and others; R (on the application of AM) v DPP and another* [2013] EWCA Civ 961

'DOUBLE EFFECT'

There is an important distinction to be drawn between the principle of double effect and euthanasia as sometimes the two are confused.

'Double effect' describes a situation in which a patient is given drugs solely for pain relief purposes. If death occurs as a result of administering these drugs, it is not the aim or intention of the medical professional but it may well be welcomed by the patient. 'Double effect' is not unlawful whereas euthanasia, where drugs are given with the sole intention of ending the patient's life, is unlawful. The importance of the distinction is shown in *Airedale NHS Trust v Bland* [1993] AC 789 where Lord Goff said

> the law draws a crucial distinction between cases in which a doctor decides not to provide, or to continue to provide, for his patient treatment or care which could or might prolong his life, and those in which he decides, for example by administering a lethal drug, actively to bring his patient's life to an end.

Lord Goff continued by explaining that a doctor may lawfully administer pain killing drugs to a patient dying of cancer knowing that while assisting with his pain, the drug will also shorten the patient's life.

The principle of 'double effect' has rarely been tested by the courts although the case below serves as a good example.

KEY CASE ANALYSIS: *R v Cox* [1992] 12 BMLR 38

Facts

- Dr Cox gave a patient suffering from rheumatoid arthritis a drug which ended his life.

Judgment

Dr Cox was convicted of attempted murder. The drug had no therapeutic value for the patient – the sole intention being to hasten the patient's death. Ognall J said 'what can never be lawful is the use of drugs with the primary purpose of hastening the moment of death'.

Example

Dr Roberts attends Edna, a patient in her late 60s who is suffering from rheumatism. Although this is a painful condition, it is not terminal. Dr Roberts, believing he is being compassionate, gives her a drug that has no therapeutic value and kills her. Dr Roberts would be guilty of murder as the drug has no therapeutic value and intends to kill the patient.

MERCY KILLING

Over the past decade there have been various portrayals in TV soap operas of a person who has killed their loved one because they were dying from a terminal condition. The question to be addressed is whether 'mercy killing' or killing through compassion is legal. The criminal law in England and Wales does not take into account the reasons why murder is committed.

KEY CASE ANALYSIS: *R v Inglis (Francis)* [2010] EWCA 2637

Facts

- The defendant's son suffered irreversible brain damage in an accident.
- His mother killed him in hospital believing he would prefer to be dead than live with brain damage.

Judgment

Her conviction for murder was upheld and the court observed that 'the law does not distinguish between murder committed for malevolent reasons and murder motivated by familiar love'.

ASSISTED SUICIDE: THE LAW

Although suicide was decriminalised by the Suicide Act 1961, the offence of assisting a suicide remains a criminal offence punishable on indictment by a maximum sentence of 14 years' imprisonment. The consent of the Director of Public Prosecution must be obtained before a prosecution is brought.

The Coroners and Justice Act 2009 amended the Suicide Act 1961 and Section 2 now defines assisted suicide as follows.

Key Definition

A defendant commits an offence if the defendant does an act capable of encouraging or assisting the suicide or attempted suicide of another person, and the defendant's act was intended to encourage or assist suicide or an attempt at suicide.

> **On-the-spot question**
>
> **?** Ronald suffers from an incurable and painful terminal condition. He asks his wife, Greta, to pass him his painkillers so he can 'put himself out of his misery' and end his life. If Greta does as he asks, would she have committed an offence under Section 2(1) of the Suicide Act 1961?

How can a person assist another's suicide?

Assisted suicide is unlawful in the UK. Consequently, since 1998, over 100 patients have travelled to Switzerland where *Dignitas*, a Swiss organisation, will assist non-Swiss nationals to end their life. In principle, a person could be guilty of assisting a suicide if they, for example, helped the patient book a flight to Switzerland or helped them obtain their medical records to send to *Dignitas* or even travelled with their loved ones to be with them at the end of their life. In contrast, the case of *AG v Able* [1984] QB 795 held that a publication of a book describing ways of committing suicide did not create a sufficient nexus between the publication and the victim's act.

> **On-the-spot question**
>
> **?** Steven suffers from a painful and terminal condition. He wishes to end his life but cannot do so without assistance. His family cannot bear to think about ending his life but have agreed to travel with him to *Dignitas* in order that he can lawfully end his life at the Swiss clinic. His daughter searches on the Internet for cheap flights and his son contacts the clinic to try and make arrangements. Will his children be guilty under Section 2(1) Suicide Act 1961 for assisting and encouraging a suicide?

The common law

The case of Diane Pretty was the first case to explore the issue of assisting suicide which caught the media's attention. As a direct result, it would be fair to say that assisted suicide has remained in the media spotlight ever since.

Diane Pretty was suffering from motor neurone disease, a degenerative, terminal and incurable disease. She wanted an assurance from the DPP that her husband would not be prosecuted under Section 2(1) of the Suicide Act 1961 if he helped her to end her life. She then sought judicial review against the DPP's refusal claiming both the refusal and the Suicide Act was incompatible with the provisions of the Human Rights Act. The case went to the House of Lords (*R (on the application of Pretty) v DPP* [2001] UKHL 61) and thereafter the European Court of Human Rights (*Pretty v UK* [2002] 35 EHRR 1).

The main arguments are shown in the table below.

Table 12.2

Diane Pretty relied on Article 2 ECHR (the right to life). She argued that the right to life also gave her a right to die	The House of Lords rejected this argument – Lord Bingham said 'The right to die is not the antithesis of the right to life but the corollary of it and the state has a positive obligation to protect both'
Diane Pretty relied on Article 3 ECHR (prohibiting inhumane and degrading treatment)	Lord Hope held that her condition did not amount to torture, inhumane or degrading treatment. Her condition was not inflicted by the state
Diane Pretty relied on Article 8 ECHR (the right to respect for a private and family life). She wanted the right to determine for herself the point at which she wanted to end her life	The European Court acknowledged that a patient should not be forced to live in circumstances that would be contrary to their wishes but a person's autonomy had to be balanced against the rights of elderly or disabled people who then may feel obliged to end their lives for fear of being a burden on others. The court held that Article 8 could therefore not be engaged. The interference of the state under Article 8(2) was justified in these circumstances

In 2009, the courts once more had an opportunity to explore the issue of assisted suicide.

KEY CASE ANALYSIS: *R (Purdy) v DPP* [2009] UKHL 45

Facts

- Debbie Purdy suffers from primary progressive multiple sclerosis.
- She wanted guidance as to whether her husband would be prosecuted if he travelled to Switzerland with her to help her end her life.

- She challenged the DPP, saying that it had failed to provide guidance that was sufficiently clear and transparent as to when a prosecution may be brought.
- She argued that this failure interfered with her Article 8 rights.

Judgment

In the House of Lords, it was held that Article 8 was engaged but the law was neither sufficiently accessible nor precise for an individual to appreciate the consequences of the law should it be broken. The court therefore ordered the DPP to formulate a policy that would be accessible to those who would want to know the circumstances in which the DPP would prosecute cases of assisted suicide.

DPP policy in respect of cases of encouraging or assisting suicide

The guidelines ordered by the Court in *Purdy* followed in February 2010. The guidelines focus on the motivation of the person who is suspected of encouraging or assisting an assisted suicide. The guidelines do not legalise assisted suicide, but merely provide guidance as to the circumstances in which a person could be prosecuted for assisting a suicide.

There are 16 public interest factors that favour prosecution, for example, if the victim was under the age of 18 years of age or the victim lacked capacity under the Mental Capacity Act 2005. There are six public interest factors against prosecution, which include factors such as the 'victim had reached a voluntary, clear, settled and informed decision to commit suicide' and the 'suspect was wholly motivated by compassion'. It is the guidelines' intention that any person would be able to consult them in order to determine whether their loved one could face prosecution if they assisted a suicide.

On-the-spot question

 Read the DPP policy in respect of cases of encouraging or assisting suicide. Do you consider that they provide a clearer picture about the risks of prosecution for those considering assisted suicide?

R (on the application of Nicklinson) v MOJ and others; R (on the application of AM) v DPP and others [2012] EWHC 2381

The case of *R (on the application of Nicklinson) v MOJ and others; R (on the application of AM) v DPP and others* [2012] EWHC 2381 is the most recent case to come before the courts. The difficulty and importance of this case should not be underestimated and is encapsulated by Lord Justice Toulson who said that the applicant's case 'presents society with legal and ethical questions of the most difficult kind'. Both Nicklinson and 'Martin' were entirely dependent on others for their care and both wished to end their lives at a time of their choosing.

The legal issues

Table 12.3

The legal arguments	The judgment
Nicklinson relied on the defence of necessity arguing that if a medical professional were to help him end his life, this act would be lawful as the defence of necessity would apply	The court rejected the notion that the defence of necessity should be applied to assisted suicide and euthanasia
Although it may appear clear under the DPP guidelines the circumstances in which a 'Class 1' helper may be prosecuted, Martin claimed the same was not true for 'Class 2' helpers, for example, carers, doctors and solicitors. He sought clarification of the guidelines. If he were unsuccessful, he would argue that Section 2 of the Suicide Act 1961 was incompatible with Article 8 of the European Convention of Human Rights	The DPP policy could not be drafted so as to include every scope of person together with the probability of whether they would be prosecuted if they assisted a suicide. The court would not address whether Section 2 of the Suicide Act 1961 was compatible with Article 8 stating that it had already been decided

The Appeal – R (on the application of Nicklinson) and Lamb v MOJ and DPP and others; R (on the application of AM) v DPP and another [2013] EWCA Civ 961

Having lost his case, Nicklinson ended his life in the only way he was able to, by refusing food and water. His wife and Lamb were added to the appeal proceedings. Mrs Nicklinson was able to do so by virtue of the judgment in *Koch v Germany* [2013] 56 EHRR 6. Lamb, who could only end his own life with assistance, argued that the defence of necessity should be available to a charge of murder. He also relied on Article 8 ECHR saying that he had the right to determine the time of his death and the manner in which to end his own life. Their appeal was unsuccessful and the court rejected the argument that necessity could be a defence to euthanasia.

The court was sympathetic with the appellant's plight – indeed, it is difficult not to be, noting that the case 'raises profoundly sensitive questions about the nature of our society, and its value and standards on which passionate but contradictory opinions are held' but the court emphasised that 'the law relating to assisted suicide cannot be changed by judicial decision' and if the law is to be changed then it must be done by parliament.

The case continued to the Supreme Court (*Nicklinson and others* [2014] UKSC 3) where the appeal was dismissed. However, the court indicated that if parliament failed to address whether Section 2 infringed Article 8 of the ECHR, then the courts on another occasion might seek to do so. The court refused to order the DPP to amend their policy further to bring greater clarity to issues surrounding Class 2 helpers.

The prospect of legislation? The Assisted Dying Bill 2013

On three previous occasions bills attempting to legislate in favour of assisted dying for the terminally ill have been unsuccessfully introduced to parliament. The Assisted Dying Bill 2013 was introduced by Lord Falconer in the House of Lords. Its principles are based upon *the Death with Dignity Act* in Oregon, USA rather than some European countries that permit assisted suicide, such as Belgium or the Netherlands, which have been criticised for their more liberal approach.

Section 1(2) of the Assisted Dying Bill 2013 proposes that if a person has capacity and has made a clear and informed intention to end their own life and is suffering from an 'inevitably progressive condition which cannot be reversed by treatment' from which they expect to die within 6 months, the patient should be able to receive assistance in dying.

The Bill does not permit a medical professional to administer medicine to a patient with the intent to cause that person's death but a medical professional will be able to prepare the lethal drug so that the patient can self-administer with a view to ending their own life. Those opposed to assisted dying argue that the Bill, in its current state, has no built-in safeguards to protect the vulnerable. We can only wait and watch the Bill's progress.

Example

Having suffered a severe stroke, Michael is unable to care for himself and is entirely dependent on others. He wishes to end his life at a time of his choosing since he is suffering unbearably and no longer feels that his life has any value. He has read the provisions of The Assisted Dying Bill 2013 and now knows that even if the Bill were to be made law, he would not benefit from the change in law. The Bill does not apply to one who cannot end his life himself. Michael would need another person to end his life for him as he is entirely dependent on others.

ASSISTED SUICIDE: THE ETHICS

In favour of autonomy

The law in England and Wales has for some considerable time recognised a patient's autonomy and their right to refuse medical treatment even where it may lead to a patient's death. Lord Hobhouse, in *Reeves v Commissioner of Police for the Metropolis*, indicated his support of autonomy when he said that 'Personal autonomy includes the right to choose conduct which will cause that person's death and the right to refuse to allow others to obstruct that choice.' If a person can decide for themselves how to live their life, it can be difficult to appreciate why a person who suffers from a painful, terminal condition is unable to determine for themselves the time at which they wish to end their life.

The argument against autonomy

In respecting a person's autonomy, it is possible to neglect the wider picture. Where one person's autonomy adversely affects the lives of others, the state will intervene. The fear is that if the law permits a person to end their life at a time of their choosing, the elderly, infirmed or disabled might feel it was incumbent upon them to end their lives for fear of being a financial or emotional burden. For these reasons, the fear of the potential, even though it may not be realised is sufficient for the law to oppose assisted suicide.

On-the-spot question

 To what extent do you agree that a person's autonomy to decide for themselves when to end their life is a fundamental right?

Dying with dignity

A person who wishes to be able to choose for themselves the time at which they will die wants to be able to end their lives with dignity. Although it is difficult to define precisely what amounts to dignity, most people sense it means dying in a way that encapsulates respect.

The doctor–patient relationship

We have previously encountered the principle of *primum non nocere*, meaning that a medical professional should 'above all do no harm'. We expect our doctor to cure our complaint. If euthanasia or assisted suicide were to be legalised there is a fear that we would lose confidence in our doctor as the avenue for our treatment and fear that he might simply wish to end our lives. In these circumstances, the elderly, infirmed and disabled may be more reluctant to attend the doctor and consequently may leave themselves untreated and without medical help.

The 'slippery slope' argument

It is argued that assisted suicide should not be permitted for fear of the 'slippery slope'. The argument is that, if assisted suicide were to be legalised in England and Wales, where would it lead?

Suppose that any new legislation would permit assisted suicide for a competent adult who, suffering from a terminal illness, had made a clear and settled decision to end their own life. Now let us consider the same legislation 10 years later. Would it now apply to illnesses that are not terminal? Is it possible that 5 years later, it may even apply where a patient lacks capacity to make his own decisions? While this may be difficult to appreciate, there is an argument that says that legislation could be open to subsequent abuse, with criteria being subjectively applied by medical professionals.

While one may choose to support the autonomy of the person who wishes to end their life when they suffer from a terminal condition, the protection of the elderly, infirmed and disabled is paramount. Although there is considerable public support for legislation in favour of assisted suicide, it is imperative that there will be built-in safeguards to guard against potential abuse.

SUMMARY

- Assisted suicide and euthanasia are unlawful by virtue of Section 2(1) of the Suicide Act 1961.
- There have been various unsuccessful attempts in the courts to challenge the law on assisted suicide.
- The DPP guidelines, which were introduced as a result of *DPP v Purdy*, are intended to provide guidance as to when a person could face prosecution if they assist a suicide.
- The Assisted Dying Bill 2013 currently in the House of Lords will, if passed, legalise assisted suicide in England and Wales.
- The ethics of assisted suicide and euthanasia focus on a person's self-determination to decide for themselves when to end their life. This has to be balanced against the need to protect society from the fear that the elderly, infirmed or disabled may feel pressurised to end their life.

ISSUES TO THINK ABOUT FURTHER

- If we have autonomy throughout life to lead our life as we wish, should a person be afforded the autonomy to decide for themselves when to end their lives when they suffer from a painful and terminal condition?
- How should we safeguard against the fear that the vulnerable could feel compelled to take their own lives if assisted suicide were legal?

FURTHER READING

Allmark, P. (2008) 'Death with Dignity', *Journal of Medical Ethics*, 28: 255–7.

Mason, J.K. and Mulligan, D. (1996) 'Euthanasia by Stages', *Lancet*, 347: 810.

Mullock, A. (2010) 'Overlooking the Criminally Compassionate: What are the Implications of Prosecutorial Policy on Encouraging or Assisting Suicide?', *Medical Law Review* 18(4): 442–70.

For the policy of prosecutors in respect of cases of encouraging or assisting suicide see http://cps.gov.uk/publications/prosecution/assisted_suicide_policy.html

Chapter 13
End of life decisions (2)

INTRODUCTION

In this chapter we consider the incompetent patient and discuss how decisions are made in their best interests where end of life issues are concerned.

WITHHOLDING AND WITHDRAWING MEDICAL TREATMENT

Patients in a permanent vegetative state

KEY CASE ANALYSIS: *Airedale NHS Trust v Bland* [1993] AC 789

Facts
- Anthony Bland suffered severe injuries at the Hillsborough Football ground disaster in 1989.
- He was left in a permanent vegetative state.
- 3½ years later the Trust and the hospital applied to the court for a declaration that all forms of life-sustaining treatment be discontinued and, once discontinued, life-sustaining treatment be withheld.

- Once treatment was withdrawn and then withheld, Anthony Bland would be able to die peacefully.

Judgment

It was held lawful to withdraw and withhold life-sustaining treatment and to allow Anthony Bland to die.

The judgment

There are various issues to be addressed.

1   If the doctors withdrew and withheld life-sustaining treatment (artificial nutrition and hydration) from Anthony Bland, would this not cause his death and satisfy the elements of murder? Murder is defined as 'causing the death of another with intent to do so'. It appears self-evident that if a life support system is withdrawn and then withheld, causing the patient to die, this would amount to murder. However, the effect would be that a medical professional would be guilty of murder every time a life support machine is switched off. In order to avoid this, the court described this act as an *omission* to act (rather than a positive act), which would simply return the patient to the position he was in when the injury first occurred, which would be lawful.
2   Does an omission, as described above, amount to a breach of duty of care? A doctor's duty of care which is owed to a patient amounts to acting in the patient's best interests. What were Anthony Bland's best interests? Although it was not in his best interests to die, Lord Mustill observed that 'his best interests in being kept alive have also disappeared'. It is not the case that it was better for him to die, simply that continuing to treat him was futile.
3   Does withdrawing and withholding a patient's treatment violate the sanctity of life principle? On first appearance, it would appear that ending a patient's life by withdrawing and withholding medical treatment should violate this fundamental principle. However, the court held that sanctity of life is not an absolute principle and where a patient has been in a permanent vegetative state for over 3 years, it does not violate the principle if treatment does not benefit the patient in any way.

The court indicated that all future cases concerning withholding and withdrawal of medical treatment must go before the courts for a declaration to be considered. Where the courts are the final arbiters in end of life issues, it provides safeguards for the patients and ensures that there is continuing confidence in the doctor–patient relationship.

Example

Having suffered a severe stoke, Sidney has been in a permanent vegetative state for 3 years. The Trust and his family apply for a declaration that life-sustaining treatment can be withdrawn and withheld, allowing Sidney to die peacefully. The court allowed the declaration, explaining that although it is not in Sidney's best interests to die, it is no longer possible to define what his best interests are as they have largely disappeared.

On-the-spot question

 Clearly explain why withholding and withdrawing life-sustaining treatment does not breach a doctor's duty of care.

The judgment in Bland has been followed in cases such as *Frenchay Healthcare Trust v S* [1994] 2 All ER 403 and *NHS v J* [2006] All ER 73 and the BMA issued guidelines in 2007 entitled *Withholding and Withdrawing Life Prolonging Medical Treatment: Guidance for Decision Making* (3rd edition) in line with the judgment in *Bland* (1993). In 2009 the BMA added that where treatment failed to benefit the patient, 'The BMA does not believe that it is appropriate to prolong life at all costs, with no regard to its quality or the burdens of the intervention.'

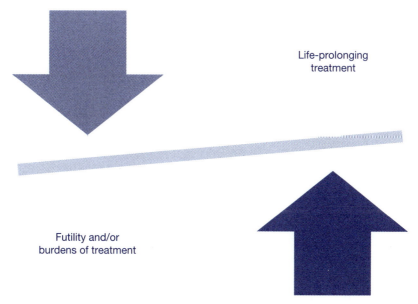

Figure 13.1

The BMA guidelines confirm that withdrawal of medical treatment is not necessarily just reserved for patient in a persistent vegetative state (PVS). The case of *Re D (Adult: Medical Treatment)* [1998] 1 FLR 411 concerned a patient with severe brain damage caused by a road traffic accident. The court allowed a declaration to withdraw artificial nutrition and hydration (ANH) given that there was 'no evidence of any meaningful life whatsoever'. In these circumstances the court held that it was not in her best interests to keep the patient artificially alive.

On-the-spot question

 Consider the extent to which life-sustaining treatment can also be withdrawn and withheld from patients who may not be in a permanent vegetative state.

Patients in a minimally conscious state

Since the decision in *Bland*, considerable medical technological advances have been made and the decision in *W v M (An Adult Patient)* [2011] EWHC 2443 illustrates just this point. A distinction is now made between patients in a persistent vegetative state (now VS), and those in a minimally conscious state (MCS). A patient with MCS is defined as having 'severely altered consciousness in which minimal but definite behaviour evidence of self or environmental awareness is demonstrated' (Giacino et al., 2002).

KEY CASE ANALYSIS: *W v M (An Adult patient)* [2011] EWHC 2443

Facts

- M suffered from brain damage.
- For 4 years she had been entirely dependent on others and had been fed artificially.
- She had been diagnosed as being in a PVS or VS state.
- Her family, together with the Trust, asked the court for a declaration to be able to withhold and withdraw treatment.

Judgment

Following diagnostic tests, it was determined that M had some level of awareness and could display some level of emotion, however limited. On a balance sheet approach of advantages and disadvantages the court rejected the application for a declaration and held in favour of preservation of life.

Example

Harold suffered an acute heart attack which left him in what appeared to be a permanent vegetative state. The Trust applied for a declaration that life-sustaining treatment could be withdrawn and withheld as treatment is considered futile. His family believes he is responsive to his family and appears to react to his favourite music. Tests show that he is in a minimally conscious state. By adopting a balance sheet approach, the courts reject the Trust's application. Continuing treatment was not futile as he had periods of enjoyment, accordingly it would be unlawful to discontinue life-sustaining treatment.

The case of *An NHS Trust v L* [2013] EWHC 4313 (Fam) serves as a useful contrast to *W v M* as L had suffered such a neurological trauma that evidence confirmed he was in a very poor minimally conscious state. The court agreed, similar to the case of *Bland*, that treatment would afford him no benefit. Contrary to his parents' wishes, a declaration was granted to the Trust which permitted it not to resuscitate if his condition worsened. Similarly, in *Aintree University Hospitals NHS Foundation Trust v James* [2013] UKS, the patient was a 68-year-old man who had suffered from a number of complications following treatment for cancer. He was in a minimally conscious state which was limited rather than minimal. The courts adopted a 'balance sheet approach' and erred in favour of preservation of life as he gained pleasure from his family and any treatment would not necessarily be futile. Following a cardiac arrest, the patient died. On appeal in the Supreme Court it was held that although there was a presumption in favour of preservation of life there are occasions in which the presumption can be rebutted. The issue for the court was not whether it was lawful to discontinue life-sustaining treatment but whether it was lawful to continue to invade a patient's bodily integrity by continued invasive treatment.

On-the-spot question

 Do you consider it ethically acceptable to withhold and withdraw life-sustaining treatment?

The effect of the Human Rights Act 1998 on end of life decisions

In the previous chapter we learned that the cases of *R (Pretty) v DPP* [2002], *R (Purdy) v DPP* [2009] and *R (on the application of Nicklinson) and Lamb v MOJ and DPP and others; R (on the application of AM) v DPP and another* [2013] all relied on the Human Rights Act to enforce their right to die. In contrast, the case of *R v (Burke) v GMC* [2005] 3 FCR 169 relied on the Human Rights Act in order to ensure that Burke would be kept alive and receive continuing treatment. His arguments are shown in the table below:

Table 13.1

Article 2 – a right to life	If treatment were withdrawn or withheld from an incompetent patient, this would breach Article 2
Article 3 – a right not to be subjected to inhumane and degrading treatment	Withdrawing and withholding ANH would violate Article 3
Article 8 – a right to a private and family life	If withdrawing and withholding ANH were to take place, it would violate Article 8

While the court upheld a patient's autonomy with regard to medical treatment, there was no right to insist on medical treatment. That remained the domain of a medical professional's clinical judgment and Mr Burke's case failed.

ISSUES TO THINK ABOUT FURTHER

- Is it ethically acceptable to withdraw and withhold life-sustaining treatment from an incompetent patient? It is a clinical judgment as to whether a patient's treatment is futile and thereafter an application should be made to the court. However, is it ethically challenging to end a patient's life simply because a medical professional considers treatment is futile and burdensome for the patient, violating the patient's bodily integrity?
- Should a family's wishes regarding their loved one be given equal weight to a doctor's clinical judgment?
- Do you think religion should play a role with end of life decisions?

SUMMARY

- Where patients are in a PVS, the judgment in the seminal case of *Airedale NHS Trust v Bland* states that medical treatment can be withheld and withdrawn if treatment is futile and it is no longer considered to be in the patient's best interests to be treated.
- *W v M* considered for the first time the position of a patient in a minimally conscious state.

- The 'best interests' principle prevails in *Burke* where there was no right to insist on medical treatment.

FURTHER READING

Giacino, J.T., Ashwal, S., Childs, N., Cranford, R., Jennett, B., Katz, D.I., Kelly, J.P., Rosenberg, J.H., Whyte, J., Zafonte, R.D. and Zasler, N.D. (2002) 'The Minimally Conscious State. Definition and Diagnostic Criteria', *Neurology*, 58(3): 349–63.

Heywood, R. (2014) 'Moving On From Bland: The Evolution of the Law and the Minimally Conscious Patient', *Medical Law Review*, doi: 10.1093/medlaw/fwu003

McGee, A. 'Does Withdrawing Life Sustaining Treatment Cause Death or Allow the Patient to Die?', *Medical Law Review*, 22(1): 26–47.

Index